the
BIBLE

the
BIBLE

Well bits of it anyway...

Mike Coles

Published by
The Bible Reading Fellowship
15 The Chambers, Vineyard
Abingdon OX14 3FE
United Kingdom
Tel: +44 (0)1865 319700
Email: enquiries@brf.org.uk
Website: www.brf.org.uk
BRF is a Registered Charity

ISBN 978 1 84101 217 9
First published 2001
Sixth reprint 2012
10 9 8 7 6

A catalogue record for this book is available from the British Library

Printed by Lighnting Source

Preface

It's been over ten years since I wrote *The Bible in Cockney*, but not a year has gone by when I have not received letters from people who have loved the book, including many from other RE teachers who have been using it in their own schools. I heard from an author in Australia who was so inspired by *The Bible in Cockney* that he wrote an Aussie Bible, again with the same aim that I had: to help God's message get across to those who would have never bothered even picking up a copy of the Bible.

I still use *The Bible in Cockney* in class, just as an alternative from time to time, and the kids love it as much as ever. The odd radio station still contacts my school because they love the idea of a Bible in Cockney! I hope that with this reprint, many more people will enjoy reading these Bible stories in an entertaining way and still be aware of God's message shining through.

Mike Coles

Contents

Introduction

Why write this book? In my experience as a teacher in the East End of London over the last fourteen years, I have often found that pupils haven't a clue what many Bible passages are going on about. The pages are full of strange words and names which mean nothing to them. It has been my aim over the years to bring these Bible passages down to earth, and re-telling many famous passages in Cockney rhyming slang has caught people's attention. The biblical language and message suddenly means something. Yes, it may seem quite humorous to read Bible passages in Cockney, but the fact is, people enjoy it! It's funny. It's nice to be able to learn some of the old rhyming slang which is not as common as it once was. But most importantly, people are not only enjoying the stories, they are understanding the message, that this Jesus geezer, God's currant bun, really does love us all. No matter how dodgy we've been, no matter how many times we've done bad things, this Jesus bloke still loves us, and will forgive us.

I know people who have told me that they would never dream of picking up a Bible and reading it, but when Bible stories are translated into Cockney, they love the idea and enjoy reading the passages. And that can only be a good thing. There's now a chance that the real message of the Bible can reach them, and that is my aim.

In my book, I have re-told nine well-known Bible stories from the Old Testament, and translated Mark's Gospel verse by verse, with references showing parallels in other Gospels. (In the Mark's Gospel section, the numbers in bold are chapter numbers and the very small numbers are verse numbers.) I have finished the book with a translation of the Lord's Prayer. One of the first questions that many people always seem to ask me is, 'Have you done the Lord's Prayer in Cockney?' Because of all this interest, and also because it doesn't actually appear in Mark's Gospel, I thought it would be a good way to finish the book.

8

Cockney

Cockney rhyming slang is wonderful. It is believed to have originated in the underworld of London in the middle of the nineteenth century. Cockneys didn't want people listening in to their conversations, so they spoke in rhyme to confuse strangers and the police. Some Cockneys I have spoken to say that this is nonsense, and that the slang was simply invented for fun, as the police could have easily learned it as quickly as it was being invented! It is a slang in which a word is replaced by another word or a phrase that rhymes with it. For example, 'pork pies' means lies (porkies), or 'apple and pears' means stairs. Sometimes the second part of the phrase is not said. So you wouldn't say, 'I'm going up the apple and pears.' You would say, 'I'm going up the apples.' In this book, I have sometimes put the second word there to help people work out the slang without having to turn to the glossary at the back.

The actual word 'Cockney' seems to mean literally 'cock's egg'. It refers to a misshapen egg that can sometimes be laid by a young hen. It was originally used to refer to the weak man living in the town, as opposed to the stronger, tougher man who lived and worked in the country. By the seventeenth century, the term Cockney came to mean a Londoner. Today's Londoners, especially those who live in the East End, still use the term with much respect and pride.

It is an exciting language, and it is always changing, with new rhymes being added and old ones falling out of use. Nowadays, if you're popping out for a curry, it's 'I'm off for a Ruby' (Ruby Murray —curry). Some of the vowels are different, usually pronounced much longer. For example, 'down' is 'dahn', 'out' is 'aht'. Quite often when Cockneys are talking, they drop their h's and g's; for example, ''ow are you?', or ''ow's it goin'?' I emphasize the point that it's 'quite often'. It is not consistent that h's or g's are dropped, or that vowels are elongated ('dahn'). You will notice in the book that h's and g's come and go, and one minute it's 'down', the next it's 'dahn'.

There is no point hiding from the fact that many Cockneys do have a reputation of speaking quite 'colourfully'. The Vinnie Jones gangster-type talk springs to mind! The strongest language I have used in this book would be bloomin' or bleedin'. It doesn't need to be any stronger than this. One can still get the feeling that it is totally dahn to earth, and having used these stories in school, there is no reason at all for the language to be any more colourful.

So, with this Cockney background in mind, I hope you have a good ol' read. (Don't get confused with 'read and write' which means 'fight!')There is a Cockney/English glossary at the back of the book, which will explain all the phrases I have used.

ꝏꝏꝏꝏꝏ 1 ꝏꝏꝏꝏꝏ

Would you Adam-and-Eve it...
it's the story of Adam and Eve!

(GENESIS 2 AND 3)

Little introduction

The word Adam means geezer, or Man to be exact. We can read how this geezer was made in the rookery of Genesis chapter 2, verse 7, an' in chapters 2 and 3 we can see how God gives 'im respons-ibilities, and how 'e then messes things up (this is usually called The Fall). Some people think this story actually happened, others think it's just a story that teaches us about ourselves and our relationship with God. Adam represents all the geezers, and Eve all the ladies. It's a clever little story this. We see how people turn against God—they rebel against 'im. They refuse to give God the glory. But good ol' God doesn't let them go. God is always working on saving us... our salvation. Have a read...

The Garden of Eden

Now, when God had made everything, the whole universe and that, he realized that there were no plants anywhere, and no little seeds had grown, 'cos 'e hadn't sent any Andy along, and there was no one around to look after the land, but there was a little bit of fisherman's coming up from under the surface which kept the ground watered.

One day, God took a bit of dirt from the ground, and 'e made the shape of some geezer out of it. He then breathed into the fireman's hose of this geezer, and would you Adam-and-Eve it, the dirt geezer started to live; God had obviously breathed fork into 'im!

God then planted a nice little garden in Eden, in the East, and it was 'ere that 'e put the geezer he'd made out of dirt. There were some bloomin' lovely trees in the garden, producing all sorts of smashing fruit. Right in the middle of this garden was the tree that gives fork and the tree that makes people know what's good and what's bad. A little stream of fisherman's flowed in Eden and it watered the garden.

Now, God put the geezer he'd made in the Garden of Eden an' told 'im to look after it, help all the plants grow, protect it and all that. God said to 'im, 'You can eat all the fruit you want, from any tree, except the tree that tells people what's good and what's bad. Now you ain't to eat the fruit from this tree, 'cos if you do, you're gonna die; you'll be brown bread the same day!'

God then went on to say, 'Now, it ain't good for the geezer to live on 'is Tod. I'm gonna make 'im a Mile End to help 'im.' So God took some of the dirt that 'e liked to make things out of, an' 'e made all the animals and little Richards. God then brought them all to the geezer to see what names 'e would give them. The geezer gave them all a name and that's how the animals got their names. So, the geezer did a good job there, naming all the animals and Richards. But after all that, none of them was a suitable Mile to help him.

God then made the geezer 'ave a real deep kip, and while 'e was 'aving a kip, God took out one of the geezer's ribs and then closed up the little hole in 'is side. He then made a woman out of this rib and 'e brought 'er to 'im. The geezer then said, 'Cor blimey! She's the same sort of person as me. She was made from a stick-and-stone taken from me, and from my flesh. She'll be called "Woman" 'cos she was taken from a man, innit?' That's why a geezer leaves his dad and finger, and joins with 'is trouble, and they become one. The geezer and the woman were both starkers (naked), but they didn't care; they weren't embarrassed.

Adam and Eve make a bloomin' big mistake

Now, out of all the animals God made, the snake was the most dodgy; really sly and crafty. One day, the snake went up to the woman and asked her, 'Is it true that God's told you not to eat any fruit from 'is garden?'

'We can eat any fruit we want,' said the woman, 'but we ain't to touch any fruit from the big tree in the middle of the garden. God said that if we eat or even touch this fruit, we'll end up brown bread!'

The snake replied, 'What a load of bleedin' nonsense. You won't end up brown bread. God ain't gonna kill you, sweetheart, 'e's just worried that if you eat the fruit, you're gonna end up like 'im, and you'll know what's good and bad; you'll know everything!'

Now the woman started to have a real good butcher's at the tree. She noticed how delicious the fruit looked, and she started thinking how brilliant it would be to know everything and become as smart as God. And so, would you Adam-and-Eve it, she took some of the fruit, and ate it. Then, she gave some to 'er husband, and 'e ate it. 'Cos they had eaten the fruit, they suddenly understood things, and the first thing they noticed was that they were both starkers! So they found some fig leaves and made some these-and-those out of them.

Later on in the evening, they heard God taking a little ball in the garden, and so they hid from 'im behind some trees. God then called out, 'Where are you, folks?'

The geezer answered, 'I heard you taking a ball in the garden. I was scared and so I hid from you, 'cos I had no bloomin' these-and-those on!'

'Hang on a minute,' said God. 'Who told you that you were starkers? You ain't been eating the fruit I told you not to eat, 'ave you?'

The geezer answered, 'Well, actually, it was that woman you put in the garden with me. She gave me the fruit, and all I did was just eat it.'

So God turned to the woman and said, 'Oi! Why did you do this, young lady?'

She replied, 'It weren't me, God. It was that dodgy snake. It tricked me into eating the delicious fruit, innit?'

God is not 'appy

God then said to the snake, 'You nasty little animal. You're in big trouble now. No other animal, just you. From this moment onwards, you're gonna have to crawl around on your Aunty, and you're gonna eat dirt and dust for as long as you live. You and the woman are gonna hate each other. Her saucepan lids and their descendants, and your saucepan lids and their descendants are always gonna be enemies. All her descendants are gonna crush your loaf, and you're gonna bite her descendant's heel.' (Many Christians explain this bit by saying that Jesus, the currant of Mary, is the descendant who will crush the snake's—or the devil's—loaf. Jesus is the one who has victory over evil and death. The bit about the heel means that because we all sin—do dodgy stuff against God—we have to 'limp' along the frog of life trying to reach our final goal.)

God then said to the woman, 'I'm gonna make it quite troublesome when you've got a bun in the oven (pregnant), and when you're pushing out the little saucepan during birth, it's gonna hurt. Now that sin 'as come into the world, there are gonna be all sorts of things that ain't all that nice. Now, despite what I've said about being pregnant, and the pain that you'll go through when the little ol' saucepan is popping out, you're still gonna fancy your husband, and want to sleep with 'im, and you're gonna have to obey 'im!!' (This is also because sin is now in the world!)

God said to the geezer, 'You listened to your trouble and ate the fruit which I told you not to eat. Now, 'cos you did this, you're gonna have to work bloomin' hard to grow your own food. There's gonna be loads of weeds and thorns that you're gonna have to deal with. You'll have to eat wild plants. If you wanna grow anything out of the dirt, then you'll have to work bloomin' 'ard. You'll 'ave to carry on working hard until you return to the dirt that I made you from. You're made from dirt, and you're gonna become dirt again, innit?'

Adam gave 'is trouble a name—Eve—'cos she was the finger of all human beings. God actually made some these-and-those out of animal skins for Adam and 'is trouble, and 'e gave the these-and-those to 'em.

Adam and Eve are booted out of the Garden

God then said, 'This geezer Adam has become like me. He now knows what's good and bad. Whatever happens, 'e must never be allowed to take any of the fruit from the tree of fork, otherwise he'll live for ever.' So God told Adam to leave the Garden of Eden. Adam was made to look after the soil and to grow 'is own food. At the east side of the garden, God put some big, mighty, heavenly creatures an' a big flaming sword which turned in all directions. As you've guessed, this was to make sure that no one could get into the garden, and ever touch the tree that gives fork!

And so, that's the story. People turned against God. Yes, God did punish Adam and Eve, but 'e didn't destroy them. God was already working on a nice little plan to save all people.

ososososos **2** ososososos

Noah and 'is Big Nanny Goat

(GENESIS 6:9—9:17)

Introduction

Noah was a good geezer, and 'e lived close to God during 'is daily
fork. He did 'is best to tell others about 'ow to live a good fork,
and please God. Now God was not 'appy with the human race.
They was a shambles, a real dodgy lot. God decided to destroy
them all with a bloomin' big flood, except Noah, 'is family, and
two each of all the animals. They were to build a massive nanny,
the ark, and save themselves.

Now, sit dahn in your ol' here-and-there, and enjoy the story.

The geezer, Noah

This is the story of a geezer called Noah. He 'ad three currants,
Shem, Ham and Japheth. Noah was a righ' good geezer. He didn't
do anything wrong. He was the only good geezer of 'is lemon.
God was well pleased with 'im; but all the other people, God was
well angry with. They were evil and violent. One day, God 'ad a
good ol' butcher's at the world, and 'e weren't happy. It was evil.
All the people were well dodgy. This is what God decided to do
about it.

God said to Noah, 'I'm fed up with everyone dahn there. I'm
gonna do away with 'em all! There's nothing but violence down
there, an' I'm not 'aving any more of it, innit? I want you to build
a big nanny, made from really good wood. You're to make loads of

16

rooms in it, and you're to cover the whole nanny with tar, inside and out. That should keep the fisherman's out.

'Now, the nanny 'as got to be 133 metres long, 22 metres wide, and 13 metres high. You need to make a roof for the nanny, and you're to leave at least 44 centimetres between the roof and the sides. I want you to build the nanny with three decks, and you're to put a big Rory in the side. I'm gonna send more fisherman's than you've ever seen. I'll cause a massive flood, and I'll wipe out every living thing! Everything on the earth will end up brown bread, but me and you will come to a little arrangement. I'll make a covenant with you (a very important agreement). Now, go into the nanny with your trouble, your currants, and their troubles. I also want you to take into the nanny with you a male and female of every kind of animal and Richard. This is to make sure that they stay alive. I want you to take a load of food with you to feed yourselves and all the animals.'

Noah did absolutely everything that God asked 'im to do. All the people living round and about must 'ave thought that Noah was a complete loony, building a great big nanny with no fisherman's around. But Noah Adam-and-Eve'd in God and trusted in 'im alone.

The bloomin' great big flood!

God then said to Noah, 'OK, me ol' china. I want you to get into the nanny with all your family. You are the only geezer in the whole bloomin' world who does the right thing, that's why I'm saving you and your family. I want you to take with you seven pairs of each kind of ritually clean animal (that means they are clean animals in a religious sort of way), and one pair of each kind of animal that is not clean in a religious sort of way. You're also to take seven pairs of each kind of Richard. I'm asking you to do this, Noah, so that every kind of animal and Richard will be kept alive, and then later, they can make lots of other animals and Richards to fill the earth again. Seven days from now, you're gonna see more Andy Cain than you've ever seen in your fork; it will keep on raining for forty days and nights,

and every living thing is gonna be done in!' As ever, Noah did everything that God had asked 'im to do.

Now would you Adam-and-Eve it, Noah was 600 years old when the big flood came. He an' 'is trouble, an' 'is currants and their troubles, went into the great big nanny to be saved from the flood. Males and females of every kind of animal and Richard also went into the nanny with Noah, just like God wanted. Seven days later, it started to Andy and Andy and Andy… I think you get the idea!! The Flood came! Think about the worst Andy you've ever been in. This was a million times worse. It carried on like this for forty days and nights. When everybody had got on board the nanny, God shut the massive Rory behind them.

The flood carried on for forty days, and the fisherman's became so bloomin' deep that the nanny was able to float. The fisherman's got deeper and deeper, and eventually the nanny started to drift along. Even the highest mountains in the world were covered up by the fisherman's, and it was at least seven metres above the tops. Anything that had lived on the earth was now brown bread—every animal, every Richard, and all the people. Basically, anything that could breathe air was now brown bread. God destroyed the whole bloomin' lot, just like 'e said 'e would. The only ones left were Noah, and all those that were with 'im in the nanny. The fisherman's didn't even start going down for at least 150 days.

The fisherman's goes down!

Now don't think that God forgot about Noah and all the animals in the nanny, 'cos 'e didn't. This is what 'appened. God made a huge wind begin to blow, and the fisherman's started to go down. No more rain! The fisherman's started going down for 150 days, and then, on the seventeenth day of the seventh month the nanny stopped floating and ended up lying on top of a mountain in the Ararat range. The fisherman's kept on going dahn, and dahn, and dahn, and on the first day of the tenth month, you could see all the tops of the mountains.

Forty days alligator, Noah opened one of the windows in the

nanny, and 'e took one of the Richards, a raven, and sent it out flying. The raven didn't come back. It just flew around until all the fisherman's 'ad gone. Noah then sent out a little dove, to see if the fisherman's 'ad finally gone down. Now, there was still a load of fisherman's everywhere, and the poor little birdie couldn't find anywhere to land, so it flew back to the nanny. Noah stretched out 'is Ramsgate, and took the little Richard in. Noah then waited for another seven days, and sent the little dove out again. The dove returned again in the evening, but this time it had a fresh olive branch in its north. Now Noah knew that the fisherman's 'ad finally gone down. Seven days later, 'e sent the dove out again, and this lemon it didn't come back.

On the first day of the first month (when Noah was 601 years old) that the fisherman's was gone, Noah took the top covering off the nanny and 'e 'ad a good butcher's around, and 'e could see that the safe was getting dry. On the twenty-seventh day of the second month, the safe was nice and dry.

God then said to Noah, 'Get out of the nanny now, Noah, me ol' china. Take your trouble, your currants, and their troubles. Take all the Richards and the animals out with you so that they will make lots and lots of other little Richards and animals, and then they'll spread all over the earth.' Noah did as God said. He left the nanny with 'is trouble, 'is currants, and their troubles. All the animals and Richards also left the nanny in their own little groups.

Noah says 'Ta' to God, and offers a little sacrifice

Noah then built a little altar (a sort of Cain-and-Abel where you can offer sacrifices) to the Lord. He then took one of each kind of ritually (remember this dicky? It means for religious reasons) clean animal and Richard, and 'e burnt them as a sacrifice on the altar. God was well happy with the wonderful William of this sacrifice, and 'e said to 'imself, 'I'm never gonna punish the whole earth again because of what people do. I'm not daft. I know that from the very lemon that they are young, they're gonna have dodgy thoughts. I'm never gonna do away with all living things again, not like I have done this lemon. As long as this little world I have made exists, there is always gonna be a lemon for people to plant their crops and harvest them. There is always gonna be potatoes-in-the-mould and heat, summer an' winter, day and night.

God makes a special agreement with Noah

God was well 'appy with Noah and 'is currants. He blessed them and said, 'Have loads of saucepans, so that all those who come after you (your descendants) will live over the whole earth. You'll be in charge of all the animals, the Richards and the Lilian Gish. You'll be able to eat them, as well as loads of green plants. I give all this to you so that you can 'ave a good ol' feed. But, you can't eat any meat that 'as still got any blood in it, because, me ol' china, the fork is in the blood. Now, if anyone kills anyone, they're gonna 'ave to be punished. If any animal kills a person, that animal will be killed. Listen up, Noah. All people were made like God, so if anyone ever kills a person, they are gonna have to be killed by someone else. Make sure you 'ave loads of saucepans, so that all your descendants will live all over the earth.'

'Right then,' said God to Noah and 'is currants. 'I'm now gonna make my special little covenant (agreement) with you and all those who come after you, and with all living beings—the Richards and the animals—in other words, everything that came out of the nanny with you. With these dickies, I'm gonna make my agreement with you. I'm gonna promise you 'ere and now, that I'm never gonna cause a huge flood and wipe out the 'ole bloomin' world again. Just to show you that I mean this, I'm gonna put a beautiful rainbow up in the clouds… 'ave a butcher's… what a lovely rainbow! This is my little sign of the agreement we've just made. Whenever it is dull and rainy, and a lovely rainbow appears, I'll always remember the promise I made to you and to all the animals, that there will never be a flood again that'll destroy everything. I'll always remember the agreement I have made, each time I see the rainbow in the sky. This is my little sign of the promise I'm making to every living thing.'

Abraham: Another Important Geezer

(GENESIS 22:1–19)

Introduction

In the New Testament (the second half of the ol' Bible), Abraham is described as a geezer with a real strong faith in God. He was a good and holy fella.

On one occasion, 'e was asked to show how strong 'is faith was. God asked Abraham to kill 'is currant, Isaac, up on a Jack; to offer 'im as a sacrifice. Wow! What a bloomin' thing to ask a dad to do to a currant 'e really turtles. What happens? Well, let's 'ave a butcher's.

God tells Abraham to sacrifice
'is currant, Isaac

God wanted to test how strong Abraham's faith was, so 'e called 'im one day. 'Oi, Abraham!'

Abraham answered, 'Yes, boss, 'ere I am.'

'I want you to take your currant,' said God, 'your only currant, the currant you turtle so much, and travel to the land of Moriah. I will then lead you to a Jack. On that Jack, I want you to sacrifice your currant to me.'

Blimey. What a thing to 'ave to do! But Abraham got up the next morning, chopped up a load of wood for the sacrifice, and put it on 'is donkey along with other bits and pieces for the journey. He then took Isaac, and a couple of servants and set off.

Three days later, Abraham could see the Jack in the distance. 'E said to 'is servants, 'Oi, fellas. You just 'ang around 'ere and look after the donkey. Me and me currant are off up that Jack over there to worship God. We'll be back a little alligator.'

Abraham said to Isaac, 'Do ya mind carrying all the wood? There's a good lad.'

'OK, Dad,' replied Isaac. So, Isaac carried the wood, while 'is dad carried a knife and some burning coal to start the Jeremiah with. As they were ball-of-chalking along, Isaac suddenly asked 'is dad, 'Dad!'

'Yes, me currant?' Abraham answered.

Isaac said, 'I've 'ad a good butcher's around, an' I can see we have some coal and wood, but where on earth is the little ol' lamb for the sacrifice?'

Blimey! What a tricky question! How will Abraham answer that one? This is what 'e said: 'God will provide one, my currant. Don't worry about it.' They carried on ball-of-chalking along.

They eventually arrived at the place where God wanted them to go. Abraham built a little altar (a little Cain-and-Abel used to sacrifice animals on), and 'e put the wood on. He then, would you Adam-and-Eve it, took 'is currant, tied 'im up and put 'im on top of the bloomin' altar, right on top of the pile of wood. He then grabbed 'old of the knife, raised it above 'is loaf, and was just about to kill his currant with it, when 'e suddenly heard the Hobson's of an angel from heaven saying, 'Abraham! Abraham!'

'I'm 'ere, I'm 'ere,' 'e answered.

'Don't hurt your currant. Don't touch 'im at all,' the angel said. 'What you 'ave just done really proves 'ow much you turtle God, an' how much you are willing to obey God, 'cos you were prepared to kill your only currant for 'im, innit?'

Well, Abraham must 'ave been a well happy dad at this point, and no doubt so was Isaac. Abraham then 'ad a good butcher's around, and 'e saw a ram caught up in the bushes. He grabbed hold of the animal, and sacrificed it to God instead of 'is currant. When 'e had finished, Abraham called the place 'the Lord Provides', 'cos

God *did* provide. The angel then came back and had another little dicky with Abraham.

'I can promise you now by me own name, that it is God who is speaking. I'm gonna bless you, me ol' china. You were gonna kill your only currant just for me. I can tell you now that you're gonna have loads and loads of descendants. There will be more of them than there are bloomin' stars in the apple, or bits of sand on the beach. Your descendants are gonna destroy and bash their enemies. Everyone, from all the different countries, is gonna ask me to bless 'em just like I've blessed all your descendants, simply 'cos you've obeyed me. Well done, me ol' china.'

After all this, Abraham went back to 'is servants, and they all went to some place called Beersheba. This is where Abraham decided to live.

Well, what a story! What incredible faith this geezer Abraham must 'ave 'ad—the sort of faith that God really looks for. In the letter from James (a rookery in the New Testament), 'e writes that Abraham really was God's china. James said that Abraham's faith and his actions worked together. The geezer Abraham really did have perfect faith. Nice one!

The Story of Joseph, Currant of Jacob and Rachel

(GENESIS 37 AND 39—45)

Introduction

You're really gonna turtle this story. In it, we read how God has one big plan for Joseph. All sorts of terrible things happen to him—'is brothers try to kill him, 'e's thrown in the nick—but all the lemon, God is with 'im and has great plans for 'im. The beauty of the story is that no matter what happens to Joseph, 'e always keeps 'is faith in God. It's a real adventure. Enjoy it!

Problems at home

Joseph was a seventeen-year-old lad, and 'e lived in the land of Canaan with 'is dad, Jacob, and all the family. He helped look after all the sheep and goats with 'is brothers. Whenever 'is brothers got up to no good, Joseph would tell Jacob all about it. You can imagine the brothers not liking this!

One of the main things that caused problems at home was that Jacob turtled Joseph much more than all 'is other currants. One, because 'e was Rachel's currant, and two, because 'e had been born to him when 'e was old.

One day, Jacob gave a beautiful, decorated weasel to Joseph as a present. It was well smart. None of the other brothers got one. They were bloomin' furious, and now they hated Joseph more than

25

anything. They spent all their lemon just cussing him.

Now, to make things worse (if they could get any bloomin' worse!), Joseph used to 'ave these dreams which 'e used to tell his brothers. They weren't any ol' dreams. He used to dream of 'is family bowing dahn to 'im. Can you imagine 'is brothers ever bowing dahn to 'im?

One of 'is dreams went like this: 'Oi, lads. I've 'ad another dream. This is what happened. As usual, we was all in the field tying up our bundles of wheat and, would you Adam-and-Eve it, my bundle got up and stood up all straight. Your bundles all made a big circle round mine, and they started bowing dahn to it.'

'You've gotta be bloomin' joking!' they said. 'Do you think you're gonna be a bloomin' king, and be our guv'nor?' Now 'is brothers really hated 'im!

At this point it would not be clever for Joseph to tell 'is brothers any more dreams. But 'e does, and 'e says to them, 'I had another dream, lads. In it, I saw the Bath bun, the silver spoon, and eleven stars all bow down to me.' Joseph also told this dream to 'is dad. Jacob 'ad a right go at him, saying, 'What kind of crazy dream is that? Do you think your finger, your brothers and me are gonna bow dahn to you?' Joseph's brothers really hated him now. They were jealous. His dad had a real good think about everything. Things were not lookin' too good.

The brothers want Joseph brown bread

One day Joseph's brothers were at a place called Shechem lookin' after sheep. Jacob 'ad asked Joseph to check that everything was OK. When Joseph got there, 'e had a good ol' butcher's around, but couldn't find 'is brothers. Some geezer came up to 'im and asked, 'Are you all righ', me ol' china? What are you lookin' for?'

'I've been having a good butcher's for me brothers. They're taking care of their sheep,' he answered. 'You ain't seen them, 'ave you?'

'They've moved on to a place called Dothan, I think I heard one of 'em say,' replied the geezer. So Joseph moved on to Dothan.

When 'is brothers saw 'im coming in the distance, they planned to kill him 'cos they hated his guts.

'Let's kill that bloomin' little dreamer boy,' they said. 'We'll kill 'im and chuck his body dahn one of the dry wells. We'll say some nasty wild animal killed 'im, then we'll see if his stupid dreams come true, innit?'

One of the brothers, Reuben, didn't want to see Joseph brown bread. 'Don't kill 'im, fellas,' he said. 'Let's just chuck him dahn the well for now.' Reuben said this 'cos he wanted to get Joseph home safely a bit later on. The brothers tore off Joseph's lovely new weasel, and they chucked him in the dry well.

As the brothers were 'aving their Judy and Punch, they saw some Ishmaelite traders pass by on their way to Egypt. The brothers suddenly came up with a plan. They said, 'Let's not kill our little dreaming brother, 'cos 'e is our own flesh and blood. Let's just sell 'im to those traders.' They all agreed, and they sold 'im for twenty bits of silver. The traders took 'im to Egypt.

A little alligator, Reuben returned to the well to get Joseph to send 'im home. When 'e saw that the well was empty, 'e got himself in a righ' ol' two-and-eight, and he tore his these-and-those. He wondered what 'e was gonna do.

The brothers then killed a goat, and dipped Joseph's weasel in its blood. They then took the weasel back to Jacob and said, 'Dad, we found this weasel. Does it belong to your currant?'

'Oh no! It does,' he said. 'A wild animal must have killed him. My little currant has been ripped apart.' Jacob was so sad he tore his these-and-those (that's what they did in them days when they was really sad or if someone died). He then wore some sackcloth material as his these-and-those, 'cos 'e was in a righ' ol' two-and-eight. His favourite currant was brown bread. He was real, real sad. All 'is currants and bottles tried to cheer 'im up. But 'e wanted no one to help 'im. Jacob was never gonna get over the death of Joseph.

While all this was goin' on, the traders had arrived in Egypt. They sold Joseph to some geezer called Potiphar, quite an important fella.

He was one of the Pharaoh's officers, captain of the Pharaoh's palace guard. Joseph became 'is slave.

Joseph 'as problems with Potiphar's trouble-and-strife

It wasn't long before Potiphar realized what a great lad Joseph was. God was with Joseph, and so Joseph was brilliant in everything 'e did for Potiphar. Potiphar was so happy with 'im that one day 'e told Joseph, 'You're no longer gonna be my slave. From now on, you're gonna be my personal servant. You're in charge of everything in my Mickey.' In a short while, everything was perfect in Potiphar's Mickey, and on 'is land. Potiphar didn't 'ave to worry about nothing no more.

Now it needs to be said that Joseph had grown into a real good-looking geezer, and 'e had plenty of rippling muscles. If 'e was alive today, 'e could join any boy pop band, no problem! Potiphar's trouble-and-strife soon began to really fancy Joseph. She used to shake at the biscuits every time she saw 'im. She fancied 'im so much that she kept asking 'im to go to Uncle Ned with her! But Joseph wasn't 'aving any of it. He was a geezer of God. He weren't gonna sin, or let his master Potiphar dahn. Potiphar's trouble-and-strife asked Joseph every day, 'Please come to Uncle Ned with me.' Joseph continually reminded her that 'e was a geezer of God. He would not sin.

Potiphar's trouble-and-strife was so desperate one day, that she grabbed Joseph by 'is weasel and said, 'Come to Uncle Ned with me... now!!' Joseph managed to run off, and 'e left 'is weasel in her German. She then started screaming, 'Help! Help! That Hebrew geezer, Joseph, tried to rape me! He ran away when I started screaming. Come and 'ave a butcher's. Here's 'is weasel.'

When Potiphar heard about this a little alligator, he was bloomin' furious, as you can imagine. He had Joseph chucked in the Moby. Poor ol' Joseph! Things seem to be going from bad to worse. But God was always with Joseph, and it weren't too long until Joseph became real popular in the Moby. His jailer put 'im in charge of all the other prisoners. Just like Potiphar, the jailer was well happy with Joseph. Joseph was brilliant in everything 'e did in the Moby.

Joseph weren't the only one to 'ave dreams

A little alligator, the Pharaoh was well annoyed with two of 'is workers, the rise-and-shine steward and the baker. He chucked them both into the Moby, where Joseph was. They spent a long ol' lemon there. Joseph became their servant.

Joseph saw them one morning, and they both seemed to be in a righ' ol' two-and-eight. Joseph asked them, 'What's wrong with you two today, me ol' chinas?'

'We've both had really strange dreams,' they said. 'We really wish someone could explain what they mean to us.'

'Well,' said Joseph. 'It's actually God who helps some geezers to explain dreams. Maybe he'll help me. Tell me what you dreamed last night.'

The rise-and-shine steward explained how he'd seen three branches on a grapevine. When the grapes were ripe and juicy, he'd taken them and squeezed them into the Pharaoh's cup, and given it to 'im.

With God's help, Joseph was able to explain the dream. 'Good news for you, Guv,' said Joseph. 'This is what your dream means. In three days time, you're gonna get your old job back, and serve the Pharaoh rise-and-shine just like you always did. Now, do us a favour, could you? Please tell the Pharaoh all about me. I've been chucked into the Moby for no reason. I was taken from my land. Please remember me.'

The chief baker got all excited. He was hoping for some good news as well. He told Joseph about *his* dream, how he was carrying three Uncle Fred baskets on his loaf. The top basket had loads of delicious swan lakes in, and all the little Richards were flying dahn and eating them.

Joseph looked at him and said, 'I'm sorry to have to tell you this. Maybe it's a coincidence that you're a baker, but something's gonna happen to your loaf! The three baskets you dreamed about mean three days. In three days you're gonna 'ave your loaf cut off! Then (if that's not bad enough!), your body's gonna be hanged on a big pole, and the Richards are gonna eat your flesh!'

Well, three days later, on the Pharaoh's birthday, these dreams came true. It all happened just as Joseph had said. But sadly, the rise-and-shine steward forgot all about Joseph. But remember, God was always with 'im, so let's see what happens next.

Now the Pharaoh has a bloomin' strange dream

It was two years alligator, when the Pharaoh had a bloomin' strange dream. He dreamed 'e was standing by the River Nile. Suddenly, seven great big fat cows came out of the fisherman's, and they started eating the grass, as cows do. Then, seven more cows came out of the fisherman's. But these cows looked bloomin' awful. They were real skinny. These awful Tom-and-Dick lookin' cows went and stood by the fat cows. The thin cows then ate the bloomin' fat cows! Would you Adam-and-Eve it? The strange thing was, though, that after they had eaten the fat cows, they still looked as awful and thin as before.

The Pharaoh also had another dream. It was exactly the same as the first one, but instead of cows, it was seven fat and seven thin ears of corn. The seven thin ears of corn ate the seven fat ears of corn, but the thin ones stayed as thin as ever, just like the bloomin' thin cows. In the morning, the Pharaoh was in a righ' ol' two-and-eight. He tried to get all his magicians and wise geezers to explain 'is dreams, but they just told 'im rubbish, so 'e kicked them all out.

The rise-and-shine steward could see that the Pharaoh weren't happy. It was then that he suddenly remembered about Joseph. He realized 'e was wrong in forgetting about 'im. He told the Pharaoh all about Joseph. The Pharaoh immediately asked to see him. So, Joseph left the Moby. He had to have a dig-in-the-grave, wash and cut 'is Barnet, change his these-and-those, and then he was brought to the Pharaoh.

The Pharaoh explained to Joseph how the rise-and-shine steward had told 'im all about him, and his ability to explain what dreams mean. The Pharaoh said that he'd had some dreams, but his wise geezers and magicians just came out with rubbish in trying to explain them.

Joseph told the Pharaoh that it was God who explained dreams, and maybe God would help Joseph today. The Pharaoh described his dreams to Joseph. He said that when the seven skinny cows and ears of corn had eaten the fat ones, they were still as skinny as ever.

God immediately showed Joseph what the dreams meant. He said to the Pharaoh, 'Guv, this is what your dreams mean. God is telling you what he's gonna do. Both your dreams 'ave the same meaning. Those seven fat cows of yours and the seven juicy, ripe ears of corn mean seven years. The seven skinny cows and thin, awful looking ears of corn mean seven years of famine; no bloomin' food for seven years! So then, Guv, this is what it all means. You're gonna have seven years of wonderful crops—loads of food all over Egypt. Then, me ol' china, you're gonna have seven terrible years of famine, no food anywhere. This is what God is going to do, and there's nothing anyone can do to stop it, innit?'

You can imagine the Pharaoh's boat dropping at this news. Joseph went on to say, 'This is what I would do if I was in your canoes. You need to find some real wise geezer, and put 'im in charge of the country. This geezer will make sure that during the seven years of loads of food, some of it will be collected and saved to use in the seven bad years. If you do this, me ol' china, no one will starve in Egypt.'

Joseph becomes the big boss geezer in Egypt

The Pharaoh cheered up. He and his top people were well happy. They decided to make Joseph the big boss, 'cos God was obviously with 'im and he would be the best geezer for the job. Joseph was now in charge of the whole country. He was the Pharaoh's number one geezer. The Pharaoh took a ring off his finger, and put it on

Joseph's finger. He gave Joseph a beautiful weasel, and put a lovely gold chain round 'is bushel. He had a real cool chariot to ride in (second best chariot in Egypt), and a small guard of honour who rode in front shouting, 'Make way! Make way!' Joseph was given an Egyptian name, Zaphenath Paneah. But don't worry, we'll still call 'im Joseph! He was given a trouble-and-strife called Asenath. She was the bottle of Potiphera, a priest in the city of Heliopolis.

Joseph was thirty years old now, and during the next seven years he collected in loads of spare food. You've never seen so much bloomin' food!

After these seven years, the famine began. It was bloomin' awful. There was a terrible famine in all the other countries as well. It wasn't long before the Egyptians were Hank Marvin. They asked the Pharaoh for food. Joseph was then able to feed 'em 'cos of all the food he'd collected during the seven years of good crops. People also came from loads of other countries to buy corn from Joseph, 'cos the famine was so awful everywhere.

Joseph's family are also Hank Marvin

Jacob and 'is family were soon gonna be Hank Marvin, so he decided to send his currants to Egypt to buy some corn. It was Joseph's ten half-brothers who went. Benjamin stayed at home. He was Joseph's full-brother, and Jacob didn't want him to be hurt in any way.

Joseph was selling corn to all the people one day, when he suddenly saw his brothers bowing dahn to him. He knew who they were. They didn't recognize him, especially as 'e looked like an Egyptian now. Joseph pretended 'e didn't know them. He looked at them and shouted, 'Where do you lot come from?'

'We're here to buy some food,' they said. 'We're from Canaan.'

Joseph remembered the dreams 'e'd had all those years ago. He then said to them quite angrily, 'You lot are bloomin' spies. You've come to spy out my country.'

'No we're not, Guv,' they answered. 'We are your slaves. We're

Hank Marvin and we've come to buy food. We're not spies. Just brothers, honestly mate. There were twelve of us once. We're all currants of the same geezer in Canaan. Sadly, one of our brothers is brown bread, and the youngest one is with our dad.'

'Don't talk rubbish!' Joseph yelled. 'You're all bloomin' spies. I'm gonna chuck you all in the Moby, and you'll never leave until I see your little brother.' So 'e locked 'em all up for three days.

When the lemon was up, Joseph went up to 'is brothers and said, 'Now listen up you lot. I'm a geezer who believes in the one God. I'm gonna let you live, but I need to know that what you're telling me is Irish stew. This is what I want you to do. One of you will stay in the Moby. The rest of you can go home and feed your Hank Marvin families. Then I want you to come back with your youngest brother so I'll know that what you've been telling me is Irish, and you won't end up brown bread.'

The brothers felt real awful. They knew they were being punished for what they did to Joseph all those years ago. Reuben reminded them how he had said they shouldn't harm Joseph. Joseph knew what they were rabbiting on about, but they didn't know 'cos they had been rabbiting to Joseph through an interpreter. Joseph then left them and had a snoop. It must 'ave been hard for 'im. When he was all right again, he pointed to Simeon. Simeon was tied up, and thrown into the Moby.

The brothers' packs were filled with corn, and each man's money was returned and put in the top of each sack. Then they headed off home. In the evening, when they stopped to set up camp for the night, one of the brothers went to his sack to get some food for the donkeys. When 'e opened it, 'e saw all of 'is bread on the top. He screamed for 'is brothers. When they got there, 'e said to 'em, 'Bad news, lads! My bread has been returned to me. It's in me bloomin' sack!' They all nearly had a heart attack.

'What is God doing to us?' they all asked.

When they all arrived back in Canaan, they told their dad, Jacob, everything that had happened. They also mentioned the fact that they had to return to Egypt with Benjamin, the youngest brother.

Jacob had a real fit! He shouted, 'Have I gotta lose all me saucepans? Joseph's gone. Simeon's gone. And now you wanna take bloomin' Benjamin from me!'

Reuben tried to convince 'is dad to let 'em take Benjamin. 'I'll look after the lad,' 'e said. 'If I don't, you can kill me two currants.'

In the end, Jacob 'ad no bloomin' choice, 'cos the famine in Canaan was now terrible. 'We've gotta go,' said Judah. 'I'll look after Benjamin, I promise. I'll guard 'im with me fork.'

They set off again for Egypt, taking with 'em gifts, and twice as much bread, to return what they'd found in the top of their sacks. When they arrived, they went straight to Joseph. When Joseph saw Benjamin, 'e said to 'is servant, 'Take these lads to my Mickey. They're gonna 'ave Lilley with me. Kill a nice fat animal and cook it.'

When the brothers arrived at the Mickey, they said to one of the servants, 'Excuse us, Guv. We'd like to return this bread we found in the top of our sacks on the way back to Canaan. Also, 'ere's some more bread so we can buy more corn.'

The servant said, 'Don't worry, me ol' chinas. We've already been paid. It must 'ave been your God who returned your bread.' Then, Simeon was brought to join 'is brothers. They was pleased to see each other.

The brothers were taken into the Mickey. They were given fisherman's so that they could wash their plates, and their donkeys were fed. When Joseph arrived, they bowed dahn to 'im and gave their gifts to 'im. He asked the brothers 'ow their father was doing. They told 'im that their dad was well.

Now, when Joseph saw 'is little brother Benjamin, 'e said, 'So this is the young brother you told me about. God bless you, me currant.' Then Joseph had to suddenly leave the room, 'cos 'e turtled 'is little brother. He ran to 'is room and had a good ol' snoop. After he'd washed 'is boat race, he came out, and gave orders for the meal to be served. Joseph ate at 'is own Cain, and 'is brothers ate at another. The Egyptians also ate on their own, 'cos they didn't mix with Hebrews. The brothers were all sat at their Cain facing Joseph, and they were all sat in order of their age, from the eldest geezer to the youngest. The brothers couldn't Adam-and-Eve how they 'ad been seated in order of age. They was bloomin' amazed. All the food was served from Joseph's Cain, and lucky ol' Benjamin was given five times as much grub as the rest of 'em. They all had a good ol' feast and plenty to drink until they was all elephant's trunk!

Joseph tests 'is brothers once more

Now, Joseph 'ad been testing 'is brothers, trying to find out what sort of geezers they'd become. But 'e still had one last test to play on 'em. It involved Joseph's silver cup.

When the brothers was ready to go home to Canaan, Joseph gave orders for their sacks to be filled with corn, and for their money to be put in the top of each sack. He also ordered his servant to put his silver cup in the top of the sack of Benjamin, the youngest brother.

The brothers set off with their donkeys. They'd only travelled a few miles when Joseph said to the servant in charge of 'is Mickey, 'Go and chase those geezers, and ask them why they've been so nasty? Say, "Why did you steal my master's silver cup, the one he uses for magic and fortune telling?" (It's pretty unlikely that Joseph did magic and fortune telling 'cos 'e was a geezer of God. He just said this to scare the brothers, and demonstrate that 'e 'ad super-normal knowledge.) "You have all committed a terrible bloomin' crime."'

The servant chased after the brothers and asked them these questions. The brothers answered, 'Sorry, Guv, but we don't know what you're goin' on about. We ain't nicked no cup. We ain't telling you porkies, you know. We brought back all the bread we found in our sacks before. Why would we want to nick any silver or gold from your Master's Mickey? Why don't you 'ave a butcher's in our sacks? If anyone's got the cup, put them to death, and all the rest of us geezers will become your slaves.'

'That's fair enough,' said the servant. 'But only the geezer who has the cup will become my slave. The rest of you can go home.' They all got their sacks off their donkeys, and put them on the safe. They opened their sacks. The servant 'ad a butcher's in each sack, starting with the eldest and ending up with the youngest. Yes, you've guessed it. The cup was found in Benjamin's sack. The brothers could not Adam-and-Eve it. They tore their these-and-those in sorrow. They was in a righ' ol' two-and-eight. They all loaded their donkeys and returned to the city.

When Joseph saw them again, 'e was furious. 'Didn't you know that 'cos I'm such an important geezer 'ere in Egypt, I could 'ave used magic to find out what you've done?'

Judah answered, 'We're right dodgy geezers. We ain't got a dicky to say to you. We are all guilty geezers, and God knows it. We are now all your slaves, not just little ol' Benjamin.'

Joseph said, 'You gotta be bloomin' joking. Only the one who nicked me cup will be my slave. The rest of you go home to your dad.'

Judah then got on 'is biscuits and begged and begged Joseph not to punish Benjamin. He told Joseph the whole story. He explained how Jacob had said that Rachel had only two currants and one of them must 'ave been ripped apart by wild animals. Benjamin was the only one left. Judah explained that if anything were to happen to Benjamin, Jacob would die. Jacob lived for Benjamin.

Judah said to Joseph, 'I told me dad that if I don't return with Benjamin, I would bear the blame all me fork. Let me be your slave, not Benjamin. I can't go home to me dad without 'im. It would kill Jacob. Please, Guv, punish me!'

Get your hankies out

That was it. Joseph couldn't control 'is feelings any more. He asked all the servants to leave the room. Then 'e said to 'is brothers, 'Oi, fellas. It's me, Joseph.' At this point, 'e had a real loud snoop. Even the Egyptians could hear 'im. Joseph asked, 'Is Dad still alive?' This seems like a bloomin' daft thing to ask, as 'e's just heard from Judah that 'is ol' man is still alive. But now 'e was speaking from 'is stop-and-start as one of the brothers. He truly wanted to know if Jacob was still alive, as 'e 'ad missed 'im so much over the years. At first, the brothers didn't know what to do. They was right shocked and scared. Joseph said to 'em, 'Please come closer.' They did, and I'm sure they all 'ad a big hug and snoop together. Joseph went on to explain, 'I'm your brother Joseph. You sold me, and I ended up a slave in Egypt. But listen 'ere, fellas, please don't worry about it. It was God who caused all this to happen. I was sent 'ere to save people's lives. What you did to me in the past were righ' dodgy, but you're good honest geezers now, and it was all part of God's plan. This is still only the second year of the famine. There's still another five to go. Because of God's plan I've been able to rescue you all, and make sure that all your descendants survive. So remember, my dear little brothers, it weren't you who sent me 'ere, but God. I'm in charge of this whole bloomin' country.'

Joseph went on to say, 'What I'd like you to do now is go back to Dad. Tell 'im everything, and then bring 'im and the whole family and all the animals to come and live 'ere in a place called Goshen. Then I can take care of you all.' They continued to 'ave a good ol' snoop-and-pry. There was plenty of hugging goin' on. It was a real emotional lemon.

Eventually, Jacob and all the family travelled to Egypt. Joseph got in 'is lovely chariot and went to Goshen to meet 'is dad. When they met, Joseph threw 'is chalks around his dad and snoop-and-pried for a real long lemon. It was a lovely sight, as you can imagine. Jacob then said to Joseph, 'Now I can die a happy geezer. I've seen me currant and I know you're still alive.'

Well, what a story! It was great to see God at work all the way through. No matter what happened, Joseph always kept 'is faith in God. At the end of Genesis chapter 50, Joseph tells 'is brothers not to worry about what they did. He said to 'em, 'I know what you did to me was dodgy, but God turned it into good so that lots of lives could be saved.'

ooooooooooo **5** ooooooooooo

The Story of David, King of Israel

Introduction

David was a great geezer. He had a real strong faith and 'e turtled God. The people loved 'im. Now, 'e may have been a great king, but even 'e made the odd mistake. He committed adultery, and in a way, murdered this woman's husband. But 'e did say sorry to God for what 'e'd done, and was willing to accept any punishment God decided to send.

David was such a great leader, that many years after 'im, when the people of Israel was 'aving problems (quite often!), they always hoped for another king, one who would be a descendant of David. One of the titles for Jesus is 'Currant of David'. So, David is the royal ancestor of the Messiah, Jesus.

The story of David is a real great read. We'll have a butcher's at two incidents in 'is fork. One (very famous) where 'e is a real hero, and the second where he does something pretty dodgy... you'll see what I mean when you read it. So, 'ere we go.

David and the real big geezer... Goliath!
(1 SAMUEL 17)

This is probably one of the most famous stories in the good ol' Bible, and it all happened when David was just a young boy.

Round about then, Israel was 'aving terrible problems with its great enemy, the Philistines. They were a terrible, violent bunch. The

Israelites were about to 'ave a great big battle with the Philistines. The Philistines 'ad their camp between Socoh and Azekah. King Saul (King of Israel at this lemon) and the Israelites had their camp in the Valley of Elah. Both armies were on top of a Jack, with a valley between 'em. They was both ready to read-and-write. This great scrap between David and Goliath took place in the Jack and Jill country in the West, the land between Israel and Philistia (where the dodgy Philistines came from). This Valley of Elah place is thought to be fifteen miles south-west of Bethlehem. Each army took its position facing each other across the valley, probably a riverbed that was dry in the summer.

Early one morning, some geezer called Goliath came out of the Philistine camp to challenge the Israelites. Now, you would not Adam-and-Eve the size of this bloomin' geezer. He was massive! He was well over three metres tall. His armour was bronze and really heavy. His Scotch pegs were huge and were protected by bronze armour as well. He was carrying a massive spear. A Philistine soldier walked in front of 'im carrying 'is shield. I can tell you now, you would not want to mess with this Goliath geezer.

Goliath then opened 'is huge north and shouted, 'What are you lot doin' there lining up for battle? I am a Philistine geezer, you pathetic little slaves of Saul! I want you to find some geezer in your army to fight me. If 'e wins and kills me and chops me loaf off, we will be your slaves. But, if I chop 'im to bits, you lot will be our slaves. So, if you think you're tough, prove it. Find some fella to read with me.' When Saul and his men heard this, they was really scared, and started shaking at the biscuits. Who on earth could they find to read-and-write with this bloomin' massive geezer?

This is where David comes in

Now David was the currant of Jesse. Jesse was from Bethlehem (where Jesus was born. 'Once in Royal David's City'—remember the carol?). Jesse 'ad eight currants in all, and 'e was quite an ol' geezer now. Jesse's three eldest currants were with King Saul's army ready to read with the Philistines. The eldest currant was called Eliab, then there was Abinadab, then Shammah. David happened to be the youngest currant.

Occasionally, David used to play the harp for King Saul. Saul turtled this, 'cos 'e often got really depressed and David's music would make 'im feel better. When David wasn't with Saul, 'e would go back to Bethlehem and take care of 'is dad's sheep. David was a great shepherd. He was a real brave lad and would often have to kill lions and bears with 'is sling to protect 'is sheep. (A sling is a little strap-like thing in which you put a stone. You then swing it round your loaf, and aim the stone at something.) He risked 'is own fork to protect 'em.

Meanwhile, Goliath continued to challenge the Israelites, every morning and evening for forty days.

David goes to visit 'is big brothers

One day, Jesse said to David, 'Oi David, me currant. Go and visit your big brothers in Saul's camp, and see 'ow they are getting on, there's a good lad. Take them some food as well, some Uncle Fred and some grain. You can take this cough-and-sneeze to the Commanding Officer. When you find your brothers, come back and tell me that they're all right. Bring me back something to prove they're OK. You should find them in the Valley of Elah (remember? about fifteen miles south-west of Bethlehem) reading with the Philistines.'

'Yeah, OK, Dad. I'll go in the morning,' replied David.

Early next morning, David got up, found someone else to look after the sheep, took all the food and set off to Saul's camp. When 'e arrived at the camp, 'e caught the Israelites marching out to the battle line all shouting ready for war. Both armies were facing each other. It all looked pretty nasty.

David found some army geezer who was in charge of all the food, and 'e left the Uncle Fred, grain and cough-and-sneeze with 'im. He then went to look for his brothers. He found them on the battle line.

They was pleased to see him. They were even more pleased to hear about the extra grub he'd brought with 'im. As they was all chatting away, Goliath, the huge geezer, appeared. As usual, he challenged the Israelites to find some geezer who would read with 'im. The Israelites ran away, as they 'ad been doing for weeks now! There was no geezer brave enough to read with Goliath, even though King Saul 'ad promised to give a nice big reward to the geezer who could kill him. The king also said that the geezer who could kill Goliath could marry his bottle, and the successful geezer's dad would not have to pay taxes. Not a bad reward!

David was chatting away to some of the men, finding out all about the reward. Eliab, who was David's eldest brother, heard David rabbiting away, an' 'e wasn't 'appy. He shouted at David, 'Oi, you little pest. What do ya think you're doing? Who's taking care of all those little sheep of yours? You just came 'ere to see a good ol' read, didn't you?'

'Blimey!' said David. 'Why are you getting your knickers in a twist? Can't I even ask a simple question? All I've been saying is that this Goliath geezer is a Philistine pig and needs a good kicking. We're men of the one true God. Why should we be afraid of this giant oaf?'

Some of the men heard David's fighting talk and they went to tell King Saul. Saul was interested to hear about this, and asked the men to bring the young boy to 'im. When David saw Saul 'e said to him, 'Hello, Guv. I was just saying to some of your men that we shouldn't be afraid of this Philistine pig. I'll be quite 'appy to go out and give 'im a bloomin' good kicking!'

'Don't be so silly,' laughed Saul. 'You couldn't read with 'im! He's bloomin' massive, and 'e's a well-trained soldier. You're just a little boy who sings and takes care of sheep.'

'With respect, Guv,' David said. 'I may look after sheep, but did you know that I kill lions and bears? If they try to get my little sheep I chase them, grab 'em by the throat and kill 'em. Goliath is just an animal. I'll kill 'im like I kill any animal. We are the army of God. I'll sort 'im out for you, Guv.'

Saul was impressed. There was something about David—'e seemed a cocky little lad, a real diamond geezer.

'OK, David,' said Saul. 'You can fight him, and may God be with you.' Saul gave David his own armour to wear. It looked silly. It was far too big for 'im, and the helmet just fell right over his boat.

'I'm sorry, Guv,' said David. 'These things feel all wrong. I'm not used to wearing armour. All I need is me sling, me shepherd's stick and five stones.' David got 'is sling ready, and went out to meet the giant geezer.

David 1 : Goliath 0

Goliath came out for his usual daily challenge, and there standing in front of 'im on the Israelite side was a young lad with a stick! Goliath was disgusted. He said, 'Is this the best the tribes of Israel can do? You send me a little boy with a stick! Do you think I'm a dog? (They did think 'e was a dog, but no one dared answer!) May my god curse you. I'm gonna chop you to bits and feed you to all the Richards and animals.'

David shouted back, 'You may have a fancy sword, and spear, but I'm coming after you in the name of the one true God. You'll all see 'is power today. I'm gonna kill you and chop off your loaf, and then your body and all the Philistine bodies will be fed to the Richards and animals. Then the whole bloomin' world will know about the God of Israel.'

Goliath didn't wait to hear any more. He started to walk towards David. David got 'imself ready. He reached for one of the stones in 'is bag and put it in 'is sling. He started swinging it around to get some real power behind it. Then he slung it at Goliath. Perfect shot! It hit him right on the forehead. It broke Goliath's skull. He fell on 'is boat on the safe. David 'ad managed to kill the giant without a sword, or armour. All 'e had was a stone and sling and his great faith in God. David then walked up to Goliath and chopped off his loaf with Goliath's own sword. The Philistine soldiers could not Adam-and-Eve what had just happened. It was their turn to run away. Saul's men chased after them. Loads of Philistines were killed and wounded. After fighting, Saul's men went to the Philistine camp and nicked everything that was worth anything. David picked up Goliath's loaf and took it to Jerusalem. He actually kept hold of Goliath's weapons.

David was a real hero. It wasn't long after that Saul became real jealous of David 'cos everyone turtles 'im, but that's all another story. In this story, we see David's real bravery, and strong faith in God.

In our next little story about David, we read about one of the real dodgy incidents in 'is fork. It involves a woman. God may 'ave been 'appy with David much of the lemon, but not in this story. Have a read...

David and some real pretty woman called Bathsheba
(2 SAMUEL 11:1—12:15)

David was now King of Israel and Judah. A great king. One springtime, the usual lemon when kings went out to war (almost like the football season, but in this case, it was the war season!), David sent out Joab (who was the big boss of David's army), and all the officers and the whole army. They went off to read with the Ammonites, old enemies of the Israelites and a nasty bunch, always up for a read-and-write. Their kingdom was to the east of Israel. This time they managed to smash them, although David actually stayed in Jerusalem, the main city of Israel.

One fine afternoon, David was having a little doze. When 'e woke up, 'e went up on to the palace roof to 'ave a good stretch and a little ball around. As 'e was 'aving a butcher's around, he suddenly noticed the most gorgeous woman 'aving a bath. He couldn't take 'is minces off her. She was a real looker! David ran back inside, although not straight away... 'e'd been 'aving a good ol' butcher's first! He then sent a messenger to find out who she was.

He found out that 'er name was Bathsheba. (Easy name to remember, 'cos she was 'aving a *bath* when 'e saw her!) She was the bottle of some geezer called Eliam, and she was the trouble of a geezer called Uriah the Hittite. (The Hittites had once built a great empire, and they had found the secret of making iron, but this great empire was destroyed by those Philistines who we've 'eard about before.) Now, David just 'ad to see her. She was stunning! He sent some messengers to fetch her. Before you knew it, they were in Uncle Ned making love! Would you Adam-and-Eve it? She returned home a little later. But folks, this is not how it all ends. A little later Bathsheba discovers that she 'as a bun in the oven. She sends a message to tell David. (Oh dear!)

David immediately sent a message to Joab, his commander, saying, 'Send me the geezer called Uriah the Hittite. It's urgent!' The army had surrounded Rabbah, the main city of the Ammonites, but Joab sent Uriah to David straight away. When Uriah arrived, David asked 'im how the reading was going, and whether all the soldiers were well. He then said to Uriah, 'Why don't you pop off home, me lad, and 'ave a nice little rest? You must be knackered!' David was being really sly here. He was only sending Uriah home in the hope that 'e would make love to 'is trouble, and would then think that the baby was 'is. But, David's little idea doesn't go according to plan.

Uriah didn't go home. He actually went to the palace gate, and slept where the king's guard kipped.

When David heard about this, 'e asked Uriah, 'Why on earth didn't you go home? Surely you wanted to see your trouble and have a bit of you-know-what? You've been away for ages. You need a good rest.'

'With respect, Guv,' answered Uriah. 'All the men of Israel are at war. It's a holy war. We have the Covenant Box with us (the box containing the Ten Commandments). All the men are camping out in the open. I can't go home to me trouble and 'ave a good rest and eat and drink. It's a holy war, and I swear that I couldn't go home at the moment. It's not right!'

'All right then, me ol' china,' said David. 'Just stay 'ere today and tomorrow, and then I'll send you back.' Uriah did so. David invited 'im 'round for supper in the evening. David made sure that Uriah 'ad plenty to drink until 'e was elephant's! He did this to try to get Uriah to go home. But this plan failed as well. Uriah slept in the palace guardroom. He didn't go home.

Now, all this is real dodgy on David's part, but what comes next was even bloomin' worse! The next morning, David wrote a letter and gave it to Uriah saying, 'Make sure Joab gets this letter.'

This is what the letter said: 'Hello, Joab, me ol' china. Please make sure that you put Uriah in the front line, where the fighting is really awful. Then fall back, and let 'im be killed!' Would you Adam-and-Eve it? What a bloomin' terrible thing to do. One minute, David is a real hero killing the giant. The next minute he's doing this. Well, let's see what happens.

Joab put Uriah in a place where there were quite a few enemy soldiers, and after a while, Uriah was killed. Joab sent a message back to David explaining how the battle was going, and reporting that Uriah was killed!

David then, quite innocently (I think not!) says to the messenger, 'Oh dear. Tell Joab to cheer up, and not to be upset. War is a terrible thing, and you never know who's gonna die. Tell him to launch a real strong attack, and finally capture the city.'

Bathsheba was obviously well upset at this terrible news. She mourned for her dear husband. When the lemon of mourning was over, David got her to come over to the palace. She became his trouble, and soon gave birth to their currant.

Now, I don't need to tell you this, but God was well upset with what David had done. God decided to send the prophet Nathan to have a real serious dicky bird with David, about all these terrible things he's been up to. Nathan did it in a real clever way. This is what 'e said.

'Now then, David. There were these two geezers who lived in the same town. One 'ad a load of money, and the other was really on-the-floor. The rich geezer 'ad loads of cattle and sheep, and the poor geezer 'ad only one lamb, which he'd bought 'imself. He took care of this little lamb, and it grew up in 'is Mickey with 'is saucepans.

He even sometimes used to feed it with some of 'is own food, and let it have a little drink from 'is cup. He used to turtle holding it in his lap. He treated the lamb like a little bottle. The real rich geezer once got a visitor at his Mickey. He wanted to feed 'im, but 'e didn't want to kill one of his own animals. So, 'e decided to take the poor man's lamb instead. He cooked it, and gave it to 'is guest.'

David was well furious, and 'e said, 'Who was this geezer? Tell me now. I swear by God that I'll have this geezer put to death for the terrible thing he's done. What a cruel fella! I'll make sure he pays back four times as much as 'e took from the geezer who was on-the-floor.'

Nathan then said, 'I'm afraid to say, David, that you are that geezer! This is what God 'as to say to you: "You were made king of Israel by me. I saved you from Saul. I gave you all his kingdom and his trouble-and-strifes. You became king over Israel and Judah. I would 'ave given you twice as much if you'd 'ave wanted it. But what do you go and do? A real bloomin' evil thing. You had that poor geezer Uriah killed in battle, and to make things worse, you took 'is bleedin' trouble! Because of what you've done, some of your descendants in every generation are gonna die a nasty and horrible death. I tell you now, someone from your family is gonna cause trouble for you. I'm gonna take your trouble-and-strifes from you, and give them to another geezer, and 'e's gonna sleep with 'em in broad bloomin' daylight! What you did was in secret, but I'm gonna make all this happen in broad bloomin' daylight, so that the whole of Israel can see."'

'What have I done?' said David. 'I've done a terrible thing against God.' David was well sorry for what 'e 'ad done.

Nathan said to David, 'God forgives you, me ol' china. You're not gonna die. But, 'cos you did a terrible thing against God, I'm afraid your little saucepan is gonna die.' Nathan then went back home.

Well, there you go. What a terrible thing David did. He knew it as well, which is the good thing. He was well sorry. God forgave 'im, but 'e did lose his kid. David later went on to have another currant from Bathsheba, Solomon, and that's a whole different story.

The Judges

Introduction

After Moses and Joshua, and the Battle of Jericho and all that, we read in the Bible about some Hebrew leaders called 'The Judges'. Now, they weren't like judges are today, people who sit in courts wearing funny-looking syrups! They were leaders of separate tribes, and there were twelve altogether.

You can read about them in the rookery of Judges in the Bible. The writers of this rookery make it quite clear that everything goes well with the people as long as they believe in God and do what 'e says. But the silly people sometimes forgot all about God and started to worship silly little gods and idols! Because they did this, God weren't 'appy at all, so 'e let the Hebrews' enemies attack them and beat 'em. What did the people do when this happened? They said sorry to God. He would say OK and send a hero along to rescue them. These heroes were the Judges. After the people had been rescued, it wasn't long before they started worshipping other gods again, and the whole bloomin' thing started again. This kept on happening again and again. The people just wouldn't learn!

The Judge would be some geezer or some woman who would come along and give hope back to the people. They spoke in the name of God, and would rescue the people from their enemies.

We're gonna 'ave a butcher's at two of the Judges of Israel, a woman, and a geezer—Deborah and Samson.

Good ol' Deborah

(JUDGES 4:1–24)

The Bible calls this woman a prophetess 'cos she always spoke in the name of God. The dicky birds she spoke were really powerful. What was 'appening during the lemon of Deborah, was that some king was making all the Hebrews slaves, so she called all the tribes of the north to join together to sort this bloomin' king out. This is the story.

Deborah an' a geezer called Barak

Once again, the people of Israel forgot all about God. God thought that if that's the way you're gonna be, I'm gonna let your enemy beat you. That's exactly what 'appened. God let the Hebrews be conquered by some geezer called Jabin, who was a Canaanite king. He ruled in some city called Hazor—not a nice fella! The commander of this king's army was a bloke called Sisera. Jabin 'ad a massive army with 900 iron chariots. He was a cruel and nasty geezer. He treated the Hebrews like animals for at least twenty years. They weren't 'appy, as you can imagine, so they all turned back to God, an' asked for 'is help. (If only they didn't turn away from 'im in the first bloomin' place!)

Deborah was the trouble of some geezer called Lappidoth, and she was a prophet. She was Israel's Judge at this lemon. She used to sit under some palm tree between Ramah and Bethel (about ten or twelve miles north of Jerusalem), and the people used to go and visit her to ask her for advice. Now, one day, she asked for a geezer called Barak to be sent to 'er. When 'e arrived, Deborah said to 'im, 'All right Barak, me ol' china? God 'as got a little job for you. He wants you to gather up ten thousand geezers from the tribes of Naphtali and Zebulun and lead them to Mount Tabor. I'll get that Sisera, the commander of that nasty king Jabin's army, to fight against you at the River Kishon. He's gonna 'ave all his soldiers and chariots, but

God's gonna make sure that you give 'em a good bashing and beat 'em!'

'I'll only do this if you come with me,' said Barak. 'If you don't come, then I ain't goin' either!'

'Oh, all right then,' replied Deborah. 'But if I go with you, no one's gonna think you were the hero of the battle, 'cos God's gonna make sure that Sisera is destroyed by a woman, not you!' So Deborah and Barak went up to Mount Tabor with 10,000 geezers ready for battle. Sisera got 'is men ready, and his 900 chariots.

Deborah then said to Barak, 'Get goin', me ol' china. God is with you, and today you're gonna bash Sisera and 'is army.' Barak took his 10,000 men, and went down from Mount Tabor. They went screaming into battle. Sisera and 'is army didn't know what hit them. They were in a right ol' two-and-eight. Because of heavy Andy Cain, the Canaanites with all their heavy armour and chariots got stuck in all the mud. They couldn't bloomin' move. The Israelites were able to give 'em a good bashing. Sisera, the little coward, jumped off his chariot and ran away. The Israelites totally destroyed Sisera's army. Not one geezer was left standing.

Now, Sisera ran all the way to the tent of some woman called Jael, the trouble of Heber the Kenite. (The Kenites were a group of people who lived about forty miles south of Bethlehem, to the west of what's now know as the Brown Bread Sea.) He ran there 'cos King Jabin was a china of Heber's family. When Jael saw 'im coming, she ran out to meet him. 'How ya doin?' she asked 'im. 'Come into my tent. Don't be scared, me ol' china.' He went inside, an' she hid 'im behind a curtain. Sisera then said to 'er, 'Give us a glass of fisherman's, please. I'm bloomin' thirsty.' She had a leather bag full of Charlie Dilke, so she poured 'im a cup. When he'd had a drink, she hid him again. He told her to stand by the entrance of the tent, and 'e said that if anyone came, she was to say the tent was empty.

Now Sisera was really knackered, and pretty soon 'e fell asleep. While 'e was 'aving a kip, you'll never guess what happened. Jael got herself a hammer and a tent peg, and quietly sneaked up on Sisera. She then put the tent peg against 'is loaf, and hammered it right through so that it came out the other side and went into the safe. Blinkey blonkey blimey! It sounds like something from a bleedin' horror film. A little alligator, Barak arrived looking for Sisera. When Jael saw 'im, she said, 'Hello, Guv. Let me show you the geezer you're looking for.' They both went into the tent, and there, brown bread, was Sisera, with a bloomin' tent peg stuck in his loaf. So, what Deborah said came true. The hero was not Barak, but a woman, Jael. The Hebrews won a great victory.

After the battle, Deborah and Barak sang a great song of victory. It was a real bloodthirsty song. This is what the Hebrews were like at this lemon. They saw God as a God of war and battles, and after they had won, they sang praises to 'im to thank 'im for a great battle. We know that when Jesus came along much later, 'e told us that God was a God of turtle, and not really a God of battles.

Another great Old Testament story!

Samson, the real strong geezer
(JUDGES 16:4–31)

This geezer Samson is probably one of the most well-known fellas in the whole bloomin' Bible. He was from the tribe of Dan, an 'e was a real hero. His parents were told by an angel that he'd be born, just like lots of heroes in them days. He grew up to be a geezer who had amazing strength. Because an angel had said that 'e was gonna be born, 'is parents decided to dedicate 'im to God as a Nazirite. Nazirites were people who gave their lives to God, and they promised not to drink any rise-and-shine or pig's ear, they weren't allowed to cut their Barnet or touch anything that was brown bread. It was believed that the secret of Samson's amazing strength was in 'is Barnet, and that if 'e ever cut 'is Barnet, 'e'd lose his strength.

One of the great stories in the rookery of Judges about Samson is how 'e killed a bloomin' lion with his bare Ramsgates. When 'e went back to the dead lion much later, 'e found a load of bees in the body, and there was loads of honey. He ate some of it. Samson made up a little riddle about this which has become very famous. He said, 'Out of the bloomin' eater, came some nosh to eat; out of the strong came something nice and sweet.'

There are many other wonderful stories about Samson. There was the time 'e killed thirty geezers and nicked all their these-and-those! On another occasion 'e caught 300 foxes, tied their tails together and set light to them. They ran into the Philistine fields and burned all the crops! He also killed 1000 Philistine geezers with the bloomin' jaw-bone of a donkey! Would you Adam-and-Eve it?

So you can see why 'e was a local hero. The interesting thing about Samson is that 'e also got up to a lot of mischief, not what you'd expect a geezer of God to do. Anyway, now we're gonna take a butcher's at what is the most famous part of the story of Samson—when 'e fell in love with a woman called Delilah. It's a great story.

Samson and Delilah

Samson fell 'ead over heels in love with this woman called Delilah. She lived in the Valley of Sorek. This was a righ' pretty little valley about ten miles west of Jerusalem, near the little town of Zorah where Samson was from. Now the five Philistine kings who were in charge of everything were totally fed up with the troublemaker, Samson. So one day they asked Delilah to try to find out what it was that made Samson so bloomin' strong. Once she found out, they were gonna catch 'im and tie him up. The five kings were each prepared to pay Delilah 1100 pieces of silver. This would make Delilah one very rich lady.

So, one fine afternoon Delilah went up to Samson and said, 'Hi there, my little lion. What is it that makes you so wonderfully strong? How could any geezer ever beat you and tie you up?'

Samson said to her, 'If anyone ever tied me up with seven new bowstrings that weren't all dry, I'd end up a real little weakling.'

Delilah went straight to the kings and told them. They gave her seven new bowstrings, and told her to tie him up when she could. She was able to tie his Ramsgates together one evening when 'e was dozing. There were some Philistine geezers waiting in the next room ready to jump 'im. Delilah then screamed, 'Samson! Oh darling Samson! The Philistines are coming!' Samson woke up and immediately snapped the strings as easy as anything. He hadn't told 'er the truth. Delilah weren't 'appy. She said, 'Oh Samson. Don't you turtle me? Why don't you tell me the truth about your strength. You would if you really loved me. Please, please. Can't you tell poor little Delilah?'

Samson said, 'OK, then, my little angel. This is how I would lose my strength. If I was to be tied up with brand new ropes that 'ad never ever been used, then I'd be a right little weakling.'

A little alligator, Delilah got 'old of some new ropes, and when she got the chance, she tied him up. She then screamed, 'Samson. Those nasty Philistine geezers are coming!' Samson immediately snapped the ropes off his chalks. He hadn't lost 'is strength at all. Delilah was not 'appy. She sulked for ages. Eventually she went up to Samson and asked 'im again, 'Samson, my love, I don't mean to keep going on. But we both really love each other, and we should be able to tell each other anything. All I want to know is why you're so strong compared to any other geezer in the whole bloomin' world. Please just tell me, my darling.'

Samson said, 'This is how I'll lose all my strength. If you get your loom and weave seven locks of me Barnet into it, I'll lose all me power.'

This is exactly what Delilah did when 'e was 'aving a kip. When 'is Barnet was in the loom, she made it real tight. Just as before, some Philistine geezers were waiting in the next room. She shouted, 'Samson. The Philistines are coming!' Samson woke up, pulled 'is Barnet out of the loom, and was still as strong as ever.

This time Delilah was *really* upset. She said to Samson, 'I don't think you love me any more. You say you do, but I don't Adam-and-Eve you. I feel a real idiot now. You're treating me like a little saucepan, and I don't like it. Three times I've asked you, and three times you've told me rubbish!'

This moaning of hers went on for days and days until, one morning, Samson had had enough. He was getting tired of all her nagging and moaning, so he finally told her the truth. He told 'er that he was a Nazirite, and explained that 'e had never had his Barnet cut. If it was to be cut, he would lose all his strength.

This time, Delilah knew that he was telling 'er the truth. He sounded really serious about it all. She sent a message back to the kings telling them that she now knew the truth. She told the kings to send their men again just once more. Delilah managed to get Samson to sleep in her lap by stroking his Barnet and whispering him sweet nothings. She then called some geezer to come in to the room and cut off all 'is Barnet. As soon as it was done, she started taking the mickey out of him, 'cos 'e was now a little weakling. She shouted for the Philistines. Samson woke up, and tried to stand and show his strength. He knew something was up. His strength 'ad left him. He didn't realize that God was no longer with 'im. The Philistines were now able to capture 'im at last. They poked 'is minces out, and took 'im to a place called Gaza. He was tied up in chains, and was made to grind at the mill in the Moby. As time went by, however, 'is Barnet started to grow again.

This is 'ow 'e died

The five kings met to 'ave a huge celebration and offer sacrifices to their god who was called Dagon. They was all well 'appy, 'cos their god had helped them to capture Samson. (That's what they thought, anyway!) They were 'aving a great time. They decided that they wanted to see Samson. They had him brought out from the Moby, and when 'e was in the courtyard, they all started taking the mickey out of him, calling him names. He was then made to stand between the two main pillars that held up the whole bloomin'

Temple of Dagon. All the people there started singing songs to Dagon, thanking 'im for giving them Samson. A little boy was leading Samson to the pillars holding his Ramsgate. Samson said to the lad, 'Can you help me touch the pillars? I want to lean on 'em.' The boy did as Samson said. The whole building was bloomin' packed. The five kings was there, an' about 3000 geezers and ladies up on the roof. They were all watching Samson, and they were loving it.

Samson then started to pray: 'Dear God. Please can I 'ave me strength back just once more? These bloomin' Philistines poked out me minces, and I wanna get me own back.'

Samson then got a good ol' grip on the two main pillars. He put one Ramsgate on each pillar, and 'e pushed and pushed with all his bloomin' strength shouting, 'Let me die with these bleedin' Philistines!' He pushed even harder, and slowly the pillars started to crack. The building started to wobble, and then it all just crashed dahn right on top of the five kings and all the people. Samson was able to kill more people at 'is death than what 'e 'ad during his fork.

So 'e died. His family came to get 'is body, and 'e was buried in the same place as his dad, Manoah, in the same tomb. Samson 'ad been the Israelite hero and, in a way, leader for twenty years.

Well, what a lad 'e was. He didn't really seem to have the most wonderful character, and 'e certainly broke all his promises 'e made to God. Some would say 'e was a crazy geezer who just wasted 'is fork. But 'e should be remembered for dying in such a brave way. Perhaps 'is time in the Moby was a time where 'e could get things right with God again, and say sorry for all the silly things 'e got up to. God is always a forgiving God, and would 'ave forgiven 'im. This is why Samson was probably given 'is strength back just one more time, and with this strength, 'e died a brave death.

The Story of Jonah and the Bloomin' Big Fish

(JONAH 1—4)

Introduction

Here's another great story. Jonah is chosen by God to go to a place called Nineveh and preach God's message. Nineveh was the capital of Assyria, which was Israel's great enemy at this point. The people there were awful, a real dodgy lot. That's why God wanted to send Jonah there—to warn them all to change their ways.

Jonah ain't goin' to Nineveh

One fine day, Jonah was walking along, minding 'is own business, when God suddenly spoke to 'im.

'Oi, Jonah, currant of Amittai. I've got a little something I want you to do for me. I want you to go to that great city of Nineveh, and speak to everyone there in my name. They're a terrible lot, and they need a good talkin' to.'

Now Jonah weren't in the slightest bit interested in doing this, so 'e thought 'e'd run off in the opposite direction. 'E thought 'e'd run away from God. Not a smart move! He went to some place called Joppa, where 'e found a nanny about to leave for Spain. He paid for 'is journey and got on board. Jonah thought to 'imself, 'Excellent. I'll go to Spain. God'll never find me there!' But God was watching 'is every step. He decided to send a bloomin' strong wind to blow

on the coffee-and-tea. The storm got so violent, that the nanny was about to break up and sink. As you can imagine, the sailors was in a righ' ol' two-and-eight. They all started praying to their own little gods. They also started throwing some of the cargo overboard to help stop the nanny from sinking. Now, would you Adam-and-Eve it, while all this was 'appening, Jonah was dahn below 'aving a bleedin' kip!

The captain of the nanny eventually found Jonah dahn below kipping an' said, 'Blinkey blonkey blimey! What are you doin'? Get up now and pray to your god for help. Maybe your god can help us!'

Nothing was working. The storm got worse and worse. In the end, the sailors decided to draw lots (like drawing the shortest straw). They wanted to find out whose fault all this was. Guess who drew the shortest straw? Jonah! The sailors immediately started askin' 'im loads of questions. 'Why is this 'appening? Why are you 'ere? Where do ya come from?'

'I'm a Hebrew,' Jonah answered. 'I don't worship all your little gods. I worship the one true God who made the land and the coffee-and-tea, and who is the God of heaven. I'm on the hot-cross-bun from 'im.'

Now the sailors was really scared. They may not 'ave believed in the one true God, but they still said to Jonah, 'That's a bloomin' terrible thing to do!' The storm was getting worse all the time. The sailors asked Jonah, 'What do we 'ave to do to ya to stop this bloomin' storm?'

'Throw me in the coffee,' Jonah answered. 'If you do that, the storm will calm dahn. It's all my fault that you are caught in this storm.'

Now the sailors was quite a decent bunch. They didn't want to chuck Jonah in the coffee. They all tried to row the nanny to shore. But the storm just got worse. They couldn't move the nanny at all. In the end, they just cried out to God and said, 'O God, we beg you, we pray to you. Please don't punish us by killing us, 'cos we're gonna 'ave to take this geezer's fork. I hope you don't mind us saying this God, but it is your fault that we're in this bloomin' mess.' They then picked up Jonah and chucked 'im in the coffee. The storm calmed dahn immediately. When the sailors saw God's power at work, they was immediately scared of 'im. They all promised to worship 'im and Adam-and-Eve in 'im from that moment onwards!

As Jonah was floating around in the coffee, God made a bloomin' great Lilian Gish (a whale) swallow Jonah. The poor geezer was inside for three days and nights.

If any lemon would be the right lemon to pray, it would be now. That's what Jonah does! From inside the big Lilian, Jonah prays to God.

'O God. I'm in a righ' ol' two-and-eight. I called to you, and you kindly answered me. From righ' dahn in the world of the brown bread, I asked for your help, and cheers God, 'cos you kindly 'eard me. You threw me righ' into the bottom of the coffee; the fisherman's was all 'round me and there were bloomin' massive waves crashing over me. I thought you never wanted to see me again. I thought I'd never see your holy Mickey again, the Temple.

'I was choking in the fisherman's. I was completely covered by the coffee, and 'ad seaweed tangled all round me loaf.

'I went righ' dahn to the bloomin' bottom of all the mountains, into the land of the brown bread. But thanks God, 'cos you brought me back alive. As I thought I was gonna end up brown bread, I prayed to you and you 'eard me in your holy Temple.

'All those who worship those silly little gods and idols have shown that they don't care about you anymore. But God, I'm gonna praise you for ever. I'm gonna offer you a sacrifice, and I'm gonna do what I've promised. Only you can save people, God!'

After this prayer, God told the big Lilian to spit Jonah out on to the beach, and that's exactly what happened.

Jonah now does God's work

God then 'ad another little dicky with Jonah. 'Now listen up, Jonah. I want you to go to Nineveh and tell all the people the message I'm gonna give ya.' This time, Jonah did exactly as 'e was told (not surprising after what's happened to 'im!).

Nineveh was a bloomin' massive city, and it took Jonah three days to walk through it. As 'e started 'is ball through the city, 'e shouted out loudly, 'Listen up, you lot. Nineveh is gonna be smashed to bits in forty days!'

Now the people of Nineveh believed the message immediately. They all started to fast (go without food and drink), and every single person, rich or poor, great and not so great, put on sackcloth. This was to show that they was really sorry, and wanted God to forgive 'em.

Even the King of Nineveh, when 'e 'eard about all this, got up from 'is nice throne, took off his posh robe, and put on sackcloth, and then sat 'imself dahn in a load of ashes. He, too, was well sorry for all the wrong stuff he'd done. He then gave an order to all the people saying that no one was allowed to eat or drink anything. This order was for all the people, cattle and sheep. All people and animals had to wear sackcloth. Everyone 'ad to pray to God, and they all 'ad to give up their dodgy ways. The King said, 'If we do all this, folks, maybe God might not smash us to bits. He might stop being so angry with us, and we might not all end up brown bread.'

When God saw and 'eard all this, 'e was well happy, 'cos the people had given up their dodgy ways and 'ad said sorry. He decided that 'e wouldn't punish 'em.

Jonah's not 'appy with this!

Now Jonah weren't happy with this. He was well angry. So 'e 'ad a little pray to God. 'Now 'ang on, God. I knew you'd do this. Didn't I say that just before I left home? That's why I tried to run off to bloomin' Spain! I know that you're a great God, always loving, forgiving people, very patient and all that. I knew you wouldn't destroy this lot! Now, do us a favour, please let me die. I'm better off brown bread.'

God replied, 'Hold on a minute. Why on earth are you so bloomin' angry?'

Jonah then took the frog east out of the city, and decided to sit dahn. It was real peas-in-the-pot, so 'e made a little shelter. He then just looked at Nineveh waiting to see if anything would happen to the city. While 'e was sat there, God made a plant grow up over Jonah to give 'im more shade, a nice thing of God to do. Jonah was well 'appy with the plant.

But early the next morning, the plant was brown bread, 'cos God 'ad sent a worm to attack it. When the Bath bun was high up in the sky, it became well peas, and Jonah's loaf was burning. He was about to faint. He then wished 'e could die. 'I'd rather I was brown bread,' 'e said.

God then said to 'im, 'Why on earth are you so angry with the plant? Who gave you the right to be angry?'

Jonah answered, 'I've got every bloomin' right to be angry. I'm so angry, I wanna die!'

'Now listen 'ere,' God said. 'This little ol' plant grew in just one night, and it was gone the next. You didn't do anything to help it grow, but now you feel bloomin' sorry for the plant! So listen 'ere, Jonah. Why can't I feel sorry for Nineveh and forgive all the people? There are at least 120,000 innocent little saucepans in it, and as many animals. I have every right to feel sorry for 'em and forgive 'em!'

What a great little rookery. In it, we can see how God is a God of turtle and mercy. He would always rather forgive and save people rather than punish 'em. Jonah should have known better, rather than just sulk away like 'e did.

Part Two
MARK'S GOSPEL

Introduction

Now then, Mark's Gospel is bloomin' short. In fact, it's the shortest. And his Gospel is action-packed. There's no time for a feather whilst reading it. Oh yeah, by the way, the word Gospel means 'good news'.

Mark's rookery gets straight to the point right from the start; 'This is the Good News about Jesus Christ, God's currant bun.' Jesus is pictured as a geezer of action. He teaches with authority. He tells the demons where to go, and he forgives people who cock things up—who sin.

Mark's rookery ain't got no time for any birth stories. He gets stuck in straight away with a geezer known as John the Baptist.

Just before I tell you about Mark, I may as well tell you a little bit about the other three geezers who wrote Gospels. They are Matthew, Luke and John.

Matthew was one of Jesus' chinas. Before 'e started following Jesus, 'e was a nasty tax collector. He weren't an honest geezer. Jesus asked Matthew to follow 'im one day, and 'is whole fork changed. The main point Matthew gets across in 'is Gospel is that Jesus is the promised Saviour, and that the Old Testament, written hundreds of years before, predicted that Jesus was gonna come along and help and save people. That's why in 'is Gospel, you'll find loads of bloomin' Old Testament quotes. This is Matthew saying that they're all comin' true. This good news about Jesus being a geezer who saves people, ain't just good news for the Jewish people, but for the whole world.

Now Luke was a doctor geezer. You can tell this when you read 'is Gospel, 'cos 'e really seems to care for people, especially the poor, and women (who were seen as second class in them days). His main message is that as well as Jesus being the Saviour geezer of Israel, he's also the Saviour of the human race.

Luke also went on to write another rookery called 'The Acts of the Apostles'. This rookery tells the story about how Christianity started to spread after Jesus 'ad gone back to heaven.

Finally there was John. He was also a china of Jesus. John's Gospel is quite deep and a little bit more difficult to understand in places. He is a little bit more 'mystical'. Some say 'e was able to understand real deep religiousy (my own dicky!) things that Jesus rabbited on about. John tells us that Jesus is the eternal dicky of God, who became a human geezer to live among us. John writes a lot about 'ow people can 'ave eternal fork through Adam-and-Eveing in Jesus.

So, who was this Mark? Well, he happened to have been a Mile End of Peter the apostle (follower and Mile End of Jesus). They spent time in Rome where Mark was Peter's helper. Peter obviously told Mark all about Jesus' fork-and-knife. Mark remembered all these things and wrote his rookery. Nice one!

Just one last thing, folks. Mark tells us two very important bits of information about Jesus. Firstly, he really was a human being. He gets tired; he has the odd snoop-and-pry. However, Mark also shows us that Jesus really is God's currant. This can be seen quite clearly at Jesus' baptism, his transfiguration (blimey, what a big word! I'll tell you more about this when we get stuck into the story), and when the poor old geezer gets nailed to a cross (the crucifixion).

Right, let's have a butcher's at Mark's rookery.

The Preaching of John the Bappy (Baptist)
(MATTHEW 3:1–12; LUKE 3:1–18; JOHN 1:19–28)

1 This is the Good News about Jesus Christ, God's currant. 2 It all started off just like that prophet geezer, Isaiah, wrote: 'God said, "I will send my messenger ahead of you to clear the frog for you."

³ Some bloke is shouting, making all kinds of girls-and-boys in the desert, "Get the frog ready for the Lord; you gotta make a straight old path for him to travel!"'

⁴ So, John the Bappy turned up in the desert, with his north wide open, preaching away and baptizing all sorts of people. 'Listen, folks, stop upsetting God. Stop sinning. Come and be baptized,' he told everyone. 'And then God will forgive your sins.'

⁵ Quite a few folk came from the area of Judea and the city of Jerusalem to hear what old John the Bappy had to say. They said they were sorry for their sins, and he baptized them in the River Jordan. ⁶ John's these-and-those were made of camel's barnet, and 'e 'ad a leather belt round his waist and, would you Adam-and-Eve it, he used to eat bloomin' locusts and wild honey. ⁷ He told all the people, 'The geezer who's coming after me is a better man than me. I'm not even good enough to untie his canoes. ⁸ I've been baptizing you with the fisherman's, but the geezer who's coming will baptize you with the Holy Spirit.'

Jesus gets baptized and then tempted
by that nasty piece of work, Satan
(MATTHEW 3:13—4:11; LUKE 3:21–22; 4:1–13)

⁹ A little bit later, Jesus came from Nazareth in Galilee, and then, God bless him, John baptized him in the River Jordan. ¹⁰ As Jesus was getting out of the fisherman's, he saw heaven open up and the Holy Spirit came dahn on him like a little Richard—a dove, to be exact. ¹¹ A voice then came from heaven and said, 'You are my dear currant. I'm pleased with you, me boy.'

¹² Then, the Spirit made him scapa into the desert, ¹³ and 'e stayed there for forty days, and that dodgy geezer Satan tried to tempt him. There were some wild animals 'anging around, but some angels came and helped the poor lad.

Jesus calls four fisherman to give him a hand

(MATTHEW 4:12–22; LUKE 4:14–15; 5:1–11)

[14] After John had been chucked in the old Moby, Jesus took the frog to Galilee and preached the Good News from God. [15] 'The right lemon has come,' he said, 'and the kingdom of God is at Ramsgate Sand! Turn away from all your dodgy ways and sins and believe the Good News!'

[16] As Jesus had a little ball along the shore of Lake Galilee, 'e saw two fishermen, Simon and his brother Andrew. They were catching Lilian Gish with a net. [17] Jesus said to them, 'Oi, lads. Come and join me. Forget about catching fish. This may sound daft, but I'm gonna teach you to catch men.' [18] They dropped everything and followed Jesus.

[19] He travelled a little further dahn the old frog and saw two more brothers called James and John. They were currants of some geezer with the daft name of Zebedee. They were in their nanny sorting out all their nets. [20] When Jesus saw them he shouted, 'Oi! Come and join us!' They left their dad Zebedee in the old nanny with some hired help and they went with Jesus.

A complete nutter with an evil spirit

(LUKE 4:31–37)

[21] Jesus and his new chinas came to some town called Capernaum, and on the next Jewish holy day, a Sabbath, Jesus went to the synagogue (a place Jews meet to pray and worship and all that) and he began to teach. [22] All the people who heard him couldn't Adam-and-Eve the way he taught. He wasn't like all those other teachers of the Jewish Law; this Jesus geezer really seemed to teach with power and authority.

[23] All of a sudden, some mad geezer who had an evil spirit in him, came into the synagogue, opened his north and started ranting and raving. [24] 'Oi! Jesus geezer from Nazareth! What do you want with us? Have you come to give us a good kicking and destroy us? We know who you are. You're that holy geezer from God.' [25] Jesus

shouted, 'Shut it, and get out of that poor geezer!' [26] The evil spirit shook the man and he was in a right ol' two-and-eight. The spirit screamed and came out of him. [27] Well, you can imagine the reaction of the people. They were amazed and started saying, 'Blinkey blonkey blimey! What's goin' on? Is this some kind of new teaching? This Jesus geezer can tell evil spirits where to go, and they actually obey him!'

[28] Everyone started talking about Jesus. The news about him spread everywhere in the province of Galilee.

Jesus heals all sorts
(MATTHEW 8:14–17; LUKE 4:38–41)

[29] Jesus and his little gang of disciples, including James and John, left the synagogue and went to Simon and Andrew's Mickey. [30] Simon's finger-and-thumb-in-law was Tom-and-and-Dick in Uncle Ned with a fever, and when Jesus turned up, he was told about her. [31] He went up to her and took her by the Ramsgate and lifted her up. The fever went and, would you Adam-and-Eve it, she started to serve them.

[32] In the evening, when the old Bath bun had set, all sorts of people were brought to Jesus—the Tom-and-Dick, and those who had demons in them. [33] All the people from the town turned up and stood near the Rory. [34] Jesus healed many who were Tom-and-Dick. They had all sorts of diseases, and Jesus also got rid of loads more demons. He wouldn't let them say a dicky bird, 'cos they knew who he was.

Jesus does a bit of preaching in Galilee
(LUKE 4:42–44)

[35] Early next morning, way before the Bath bun came up, Jesus got up and left the Mickey Mouse. He found a nice quiet and lonely spot, and he prayed. [36] But Simon and his chinas went out looking for him. [37] When they found him, they said, 'Oi, Jesus! Everyone's butcher's hooking for ya.'

³⁸ Jesus said, 'Let's go and visit a few other towns round 'ere. I've gotta preach in them as well, 'cos that's why I came, see?' ³⁹ So he went all over the place, all round Galilee, preaching in the synagogue and telling demons where to go left, right and centre.

Jesus heals some geezer
(MATTHEW 8:1–4; LUKE 5:12–16)

⁴⁰ There was this geezer who had leprosy (some dodgy skin disease), and he came to Jesus, fell on his biscuits and said, 'If you want to, please make me clean.' ⁴¹ Jesus felt really sorry for the geezer. He stretched out his Ramsgate and touched him. 'I do want to,' Jesus said. 'Be clean!' ⁴² Well would you Adam-and-Eve it, the disease left the fella immediately and he was clean! ⁴³ Jesus then said quite seriously to him, as he sent him on his way, ⁴⁴ 'Now don't tell anyone about this, will ya? Go straight to the priest and he'll check you out, and then make sure you offer up a little sacrifice that Moses talked about and that'll prove to all the people that you're clean.' ⁴⁵ But the geezer was so happy, he started to tell people everywhere what had happened. In fact, he rabbit-and-porked about it so much that Jesus couldn't go into town publicly. He 'ad to stay out in the country, and people came to see him from all over the place.

Jesus heals another geezer who's paralysed
(MATTHEW 9:1-8; LUKE 5:17–26)

2 When 'e went back to Capernaum a few days later, the news soon spread that he was back home. ² So, as usual, loads of people gathered, and there weren't no room left, not even in front of the old Rory. Now, Jesus was 'aving a good ol' preach to them about the Truth, ³ when four geezers arrived, carrying a paralysed man. ⁴ There were so many bloomin' people, that these four geezers couldn't get the paralysed man to Jesus. So this is what they did: they took away the bloomin' roof right above where Jesus was preaching. Once they'd made this opening, they lowered the paralysed geezer dahn lying on his dog-and-cat. [5] Now Jesus could see how much faith these four geezers had, and so he said to the paralysed bloke, 'My currant, your sins are forgiven.' [6] Well, some teachers of the Law who happened to be 'anging around were not happy with this and they started saying, [7] 'Who on earth does this Jesus geezer think he is, talking like this? This is terrible. It's blasphemy! (A terrible thing to do against God.) Only God can forgive sins!'

[8] Jesus weren't daft—'e knew what they were thinking, and so 'e said to 'em, 'What are you lot goin' on about? [9] Now think about it. What would be easier for me to say to this poor paralysed geezer, "Your sins are forgiven," or, "Get up, pick up your dog, and go and ball-and-chalk?" [10] I'll show you lot, then, that the currant of Man has got the power and authority on earth to forgive sins.' Jesus then said to the paralysed geezer, [11] 'Now then, me ol' china. Get up, pick up your dog and go home!' [12] As everyone watched, the geezer got up, picked up his dog and ran off. Well, the people couldn't Adam-and-Eve it. They were amazed. They started praising God, and they said, 'Blimey! We've never seen nothing like this before!'

Jesus calls some bloke called Levi to be part of the gang

(MATTHEW 9:9–13; LUKE 5:27–32)

[13] Jesus then took off and went back to the seaside—Lake Galilee to be exact. Yet again, a crowd came to him, and he started to teach them. [14] As 'e was strolling along, he saw a dodgy ol' tax collector. His name was Levi, Alphaeus's currant. Levi was sitting in his office, ripping people off as most tax collectors did in them days. Then, would you Adam-and-Eve it, Jesus said to him, 'Oi, Levi! Come and follow me.' Well, Levi left his office and followed him. [15] Later on, Jesus had a bite to eat in Levi's Mickey. There were loads of dodgy people at the Cain-and-Abel—tax collectors and all sorts—sitting there with Jesus and his disciples. [16] As usual, some teachers of the

Law (they were Pharisees) were quite disgusted that Jesus was mixing with all these scum of the earth. 'How can 'e eat with such people?' they said. The dicky Pharisee means 'righteous one'. These Pharisee geezers followed the Jewish laws really strictly. Many of them thought they was better than everyone else. They thought they was really flash. Most of 'em were righ' dodgy geezers, and Jesus didn't 'ave much time for them.

[17] Jesus heard them moaning and said, 'Those people who are well and healthy don't need a doctor, only those who are Tom-and-Dick. I haven't come here to call respectable people, but all the dodgy people and the outcasts.'

The Pharisees make a fuss about fasting (going without food)

(MATTHEW 9:14–17; LUKE 5:33–39)

[18] Now John the Bappy's gang and some Pharisees were fasting, and some people came up to Jesus and asked, 'Oi! How come John the Bappy's disciples and the Pharisees and their gang are all fasting, but your chinas are not?'

[19] Jesus said, 'If you went to a wedding, would you go along and have no food, but just sit there and fast? Of course you bloomin wouldn't! While the bridegroom's still there, that's the last thing you'd do. [20] But, listen here. There'll come a day when the bridegroom is taken away. Then you'll have to fast.

[21] 'If you're trying to patch up your old weasel, you don't use a new piece of cloth, do ya? If you do, the new patch will shrink and it'll tear off some of the old cloth, and then you'll end up with an even bigger hole. [22] Also, who in their right mind would pour new rise-and-shine into used wineskins? No one, cos the rise-and-shine will burst the skins, and then you'd have no rise-and-shine or wineskins. So, you use your loaf and pour the new rise-and-shine into fresh wineskins.'

The Pharisees now make a fuss about the Sabbath
(MATTHEW 12:1–8; LUKE 6:1–5)

23 Jesus was strolling through some ol' cornfields on the Sabbath. (This was the Jewish holy day of rest. There were all sorts of strict rules about what you could and couldn't do.) As Jesus' little gang strolled along with him, they started to pick some corn. 24 As usual, the Pharisees started making a fuss and they said to Jesus, 'Now listen here, matey. It's against our Law for your gang of disciples to be doing that on the Sabbath!' 25 Jesus replied, 'Did you never read about David when he was peckish and needed something to eat? He and his men were Hank Marvin, 26 so he went into God's Mickey Mouse and ate some of the Uncle Fred which was offered to God. This all happened when some geezer called Abiathar was the High Priest. Our Law states that only the priests may eat this Uncle Fred. But, David ate it, and 'e even gave it to his men.' 27 Jesus then finished off by saying, 'The Sabbath was made for people, not people for the Sabbath. 28 The currant of Man is the Lord, even Lord of the ol' Sabbath.'

The geezer with a paralysed Ramsgate
(MATTHEW 12:9–14; LUKE 6:6–11)

3 As usual, Jesus went into the synagogue, and there was some geezer with a dodgy looking Ramsgate; it was paralysed, 2 and surprise, surprise, there were some people there keeping a close eye on Jesus, checking to see whether he'd heal this bloke on the Sabbath, 'cos they wanted to get Jesus into a spot of bother. 3 Jesus said to the bloke with the dodgy hand, 'Come over here, son.' 4 Jesus then said to all the people, 'What does our Law say about what we can do on the Sabbath? Should we help people or cause them a bit of grief? Should we save people or kill them?' The people didn't say a bloomin' thing. 5 Jesus was not happy with them. He felt sorry for the poor lot, because they were such a stubborn bunch and were so wrong. Jesus said to the geezer with the dodgy hand, 'Stretch out your Ramsgate, mate.' He did so, and it got better. 6 The

Pharisees stormed out and left the synagogue, and they met up with some of Herod's mob, and they all made plans to do away with Jesus for good!

A load of people by the lake

[7] Jesus went with his chinas to the seaside, by Lake Galilee. A massive crowd followed him. [8] They came from all over the shop—Galilee, Judea, Jerusalem, from Idumea (funny name), from the east side of the Jordan and from Tyre and Sidon. In other words, a hell of a lot of people were there! They had all come to see Jesus 'cos they'd heard what he'd been up to, preaching and healing and all that. [9] The crowd was so bloomin' big that Jesus told his disciples to get a nanny ready for him, so that the people wouldn't crush him. [10] He had healed loads of people, and all those who were Tom kept pushing their way to him like a rugby scrum, just to be able to touch him. [11] Some of the people had those dodgy evil spirits in them, and when they saw Jesus they fell dahn before him crying out, 'You are the currant of God!' [12] Jesus very seriously told the evil spirits not to tell anyone who he was.

Jesus ends up with twelve close mates (the apostles)

(MATTHEW 10:1–4; LUKE 6:12–16)

[13] Jesus then went up the Jack and called to himself the men he wanted to give him a hand. They came to him. [14] He chose twelve, and 'e called them apostles. (This means one who is 'sent out' to preach.) 'You lot are gonna be with me,' he said to them. 'You will be sent out to preach, [15] and you'll have authority to slap a few demons about and drive them out of people.'

[16] These are the twelve geezers he chose: Simon (Jesus gave him a new name of Peter, the Salford Dock); [17] James and his brother John, the sons of that geezer called Zebedee (Jesus gave them the surname Boanerges, which means 'Men of Thunder'); [18] Andrew, Philip, Bartholomew, Matthew, Thomas, James son of Alphaeus, Thaddaeus,

Simon, the geezer who fought Romans, 'cos he was a real patriotic bloke, [19] and Judas Iscariot, who was the sad bloke who grassed on Jesus a little later in the story.

Jesus and Beelzebul (the chief demon geezer!)
(MATTHEW 12:22–32; LUKE 11:14–23; 12:10)

[20] Jesus then went back home. Yes, you've guessed it, another large crowd gathered, and Jesus and his gang had no time to eat. [21] When all his family heard about this, they went out to try and grab hold of him, because loads of people said he'd gone barmy!

[22] Some important geezers from Jerusalem, who were teachers of the Law, started saying that Jesus had Beelzebul in him. 'It's the chief of the demons who gives him the power to drive them out.'

[23] Jesus called them over so that 'e could have a chat with them. He spoke to them in parables. 'Oi, you daft lot! How can Satan drive out Satan? [24] If a country was to divide itself into small groups, and they started to fight each other, the bloomin country would be in a right old two-and-eight, and would fall apart. [25] It's the same with a family. If a family divided itself into small groups and they started to fight each other, the family would end up in a right ol' mess. [26] So folks, if Satan's kingdom divides into groups, it won't last, it'll be finished.

[27] 'You can't break into some strong geezer's house and nick all his stuff unless you tie the geezer up first, then you can half-inch all his stuff.

[28] 'I'll tell you something, everyone can be forgiven their sins, and all the nasty things people say can be forgiven. [29] But, let me tell you this. Anybody who says anything dodgy or evil against the Holy Spirit will never, ever be forgiven, because this is an eternal sin—it'll last for ever!' [30] (Now the reason Jesus said this was because some sad people kept saying, 'He's got an evil spirit in him.')

Jesus' finger and brothers
(MATTHEW 12:46–50; LUKE 8:19–21)

31 Then Jesus' finger and brothers turned up. They all stood outside the Mickey and sent in a message, asking for him. 32 Some people were sat round Jesus, and they said to 'im, 'Look, your finger, skin-and-blisters and brothers are outside, and they want to see ya.'

33 Jesus said to them, 'Who's my mum? Who are my brothers?' 34 He had a good butcher's at all the people sitting round him and said, 'Have a butcher's! Here's me mum and me brothers! 35 Whoever does what God wants 'im or 'er to do is me brother, me skin-and-blister, me finger.'

The parable of the sower
(MATTHEW 13:1–9; LUKE 8:4–8)

4 As 'e usually did, Jesus started to teach dahn by Lake Galilee. Such a massive crowd gathered, that 'e had to get into a nanny, and 'e sat dahn in it. The nanny was out in the fisherman's, and the massive crowd were standing on the shore at the fisherman's edge. 2 He used parables to teach them lots of stuff, and 'e said to 'em:

3 'Listen up! There was once this geezer who went out to sow some corn, as you do. 4 As 'e was scattering all the seed in the field, some of it fell along the frog, and all the little Richards came and ate the seed up. 5 Some of the seed fell on some rocky ground, and there was hardly any soil there. The little seed sprouted really quickly, because the soil was not very deep. 6 Then, the ol' Bath bun came up, and it burnt the young plants; and 'cos the roots hadn't grown very deep, the little plants all dried up. 7 Some of the seed fell into some thorn bushes, which grew up and choked the plants, and they didn't produce any corn. 8 But, folks, some seeds fell in good soil, and the plants sprouted, they grew, and produced loads of corn; some had thirty grains, some had sixty, and would you Adam-and-Eve it, some had a hundred!'

9 And to finish off Jesus said, 'Now listen up then, if you've got ears!'

The whole point of the parables
(MATTHEW 13:10–17; LUKE 8:9–10)

[10] When Jesus was on 'is Tod, some of the people who'd 'eard 'im came to him with the twelve disciples. They wanted to know what on earth he'd been talking about in his parables. [11] 'Now listen 'ere. You've been given the secret of the kingdom of God,' Jesus told them. 'But all the others, those on the outside, hear everything in parables. [12] So that, "they may have a butcher's, but can't see; they may have a good ol' listen, but they won't have a bloomin' clue about what's being said. 'Cos if they did, they'd turn to God, wouldn't they, and then 'e'd forgive them."'

Jesus has to explain the bloomin' parable of the sower
(MATTHEW 13:18–23; LUKE 8:11–15)

[13] Jesus then asked them all, 'Don't you have a clue what this parable is on about? How on earth are you ever going to understand any parable that I tell you? Now listen up, and I'll tell you what the parable of the sower is all about. [14] The geezer who does the sowing is actually sowing God's message. [15] Now some people are like the seeds that fall along the frog—as soon as they hear the old message, dodgy old Satan comes along and takes it away. [16] Other people are like the seeds that fall on the rocky ground. As soon as they hear the message, they're made up with it. [17] But it doesn't sink in very deeply, and they don't last long. So when a bit of hassle comes along because of the message, they soon can't hack it and give up. [18] And other people are like the seeds which are sown in the thorn bushes. These people hear the message, [19] but they're so concerned about everyday worries, making a bit of bread and all that, that the message becomes choked, and they get nowhere; they don't bear no fruit! [20] But then you get those people who are like the seed which is sown in the good soil. These people hear the message, and they accept it, God bless 'em. These people are successful, and they bear fruit: some thirty, some sixty, and blimey, some a hundred!'

The merry-and-bright under a bowl
(LUKE 8:16–18)

²¹ Jesus carried on, 'Does anyone ever bring in a merry and shove it under a bowl or an Uncle Ned? He'd obviously put it on a lampstand, wouldn't 'e? ²² Whatever has been hidden away will soon come out into the open, and whatever is covered up will soon be uncovered. ²³ Now, whoever 'as got ears, I suggest you listen up!'

²⁴ Jesus also said to them, 'Listen up, you lot! The way you judge others is exactly the way God is gonna judge you, but he'll be a lot more strict about it.

²⁵ 'The person who has something is gonna be given a lot more, and the fella who has nothing is gonna lose even what little he's got.'

The parable of the growing seed

²⁶ Jesus carried on by saying, 'The kingdom of God is like this. A geezer scatters his seed in a field, like ya do. ²⁷ He has a feather at night, and is up and about during the day, and during all that time his little seeds are happily sprouting and growing. Yet this geezer hasn't a bloomin' clue how it all happens. ²⁸ Now, the soil obviously makes the plants grow and then bear fruit; first the tender stalk appears, then the ear, and then, Bob's your uncle, finally the ear full of corn. ²⁹ When the corn is juicy and ripe, the geezer starts cutting it with his sickle, because now it's harvest time.'

The parable of the mustard seed
(MATTHEW 13:31–32, 34; LUKE 13:18–19)

³⁰ 'OK, then. Let's try this little parable to help explain to you what the kingdom of God is like,' said Jesus. ³¹ 'It's like this. Another geezer takes a mustard seed, probably the smallest little seed in the whole wide world, and 'e plants it in the ol' safe-and-sound. ³² After a little while, it grows up and becomes a massive plant. Its branches are so bloomin' big that little Richards make their nests in its shade.'

³³ Jesus told loads of other parables like this to the people, to get his message across. He told them as much as he thought they could understand. ³⁴ Jesus only spoke using parables, but when 'e was on his Jack with his chinas, the disciples, he would explain all his parables and teachings to them.

Blinkey blonkey blimey! Jesus calms a storm
(MATTHEW 8:23–27; LUKE 8:22–25)

³⁵ Later on that very evening, Jesus said to his chinas, 'Let's go to the other side of the lake.' ³⁶ So they left all the people, and the disciples got into the nanny. Jesus was already sat there. There were quite a few others nannies there too. ³⁷ And then, would you Adam-and-Eve it, a huge wind started to blow up, and the waves got so bloomin' big, that they began to spill into the nanny. It got to the stage where the nanny was almost gonna fill up with fisherman's. ³⁸ Despite all this, Jesus was at the back of the boat 'aving a kip, lying there with his loaf on a pillow. The disciples woke him up and said, 'Teacher, we're about to die. Don't you care?' ³⁹ Jesus got up from his little kip and shouted at the wind, 'Oi, be quiet!' and he said to the massive old waves, 'Oi, be still!' The wind suddenly died dahn, and it became really calm. ⁴⁰ Jesus then said to his disciples, 'What is it with you lot? Why were you all so frightened? Do you still not have faith?' ⁴¹ But, the disciples were in a right ol' two-an'-eight. They said to each other, 'Who is this Jesus geezer? Even the bloomin' wind and waves obey him!'

Jesus heals some geezer with more of them dodgy evil spirits
(MATTHEW 8:28–34; LUKE 8:26–39)

5 Jesus and his gang arrived on the other side of Lake Galilee, in an area called Gerasa. ² No sooner had Jesus stepped out of the ol' nanny, when some odd looking geezer came to meet him who had just come from some burial caves. This fella had an evil spirit in him, ³ and he lived among all the tombs and graves. No one was able to keep him chained up any more. ⁴ Loads of times his Germans and plates had been chained, but every time he was able to break the chains, and 'e smashed the irons on his plates. No geezer could control him 'cos he was so bloomin' strong. ⁵ Every day and all night he wandered among the tombs and through the Jack-and-Jills, screaming and cutting himself with stones like a complete madman!

⁶ Now 'e was a fair old distance away when 'e saw Jesus, so 'e ran, fell on 'is biscuits before 'im, ⁷ and screamed, making an awful bleedin' racket, 'Jesus, Son of the Most High God! What on earth do you want with me? Now, I beg ya, for God's sake, please don't have a go at me, or punish me!' ⁸ (The only reason 'e said this was because Jesus had said, 'Evil spirit, come out of this geezer, now!')

⁹ Jesus then asked him, 'So, what's your name?'

The geezer answered, 'My name is "Mob". This is because there are loads of us!' ¹⁰ The geezer kept on begging Jesus not to send these dodgy evil spirits out of this area.

¹¹ Now there just happened to be a load of pigs near by, stuffing their faces as they do, on the hillside. ¹² The evil spirits begged Jesus, 'Please send us into the pigs. Come on, mate, let us go into the pigs.' ¹³ Jesus let them go, and the spirits left the poor geezer and went into the pigs. Then, would you Adam-and-Eve it, the whole herd of pigs—and we're talking about a thousand in all—suddenly ran over the side of the bloomin' cliff, and they were all drowned!

¹⁴ The geezers who had been looking after the pigs ran away (it's not bloomin' surprising!) and they told everyone in the town and the farms the news about what they'd seen. Not surprising, a load of people went out to see what had happened, ¹⁵ and when they got to Jesus, they saw the poor geezer who used to have the mob of demons in him. He was sat there, quite happy, and quite normal again; not all that ranting and raving like a madman. He also had some decent clothing on. The people were quite afraid. ¹⁶ All those who had seen what happened with the demons and pigs and all that, told the people everything. ¹⁷ Having heard all this they

asked Jesus to leave their patch, and go and cause some bother elsewhere.

[18] As Jesus was stepping in to the nanny, the geezer who had had the demons shouted and begged, 'Oi, Jesus! Let us come with you please, me ol' china!' [19] But Jesus wouldn't let 'im. Jesus told the man to go back to his family. 'Tell your folks how much the Lord has done for you, and what a kind old sort he is.'

[20] The geezer left and travelled through the Ten Towns. (These ten towns were in a large area called the Decapolis, south-east of Galilee, east of the River Jordan.) He told everyone what this Jesus geezer had done for him. All those who heard him were gob-smacked and amazed.

A geezer called Jairus and his bottle-of-water and some woman who touches Jesus' weasel

(MATTHEW 9:18–26; LUKE 8:40–56)

[21] Jesus travelled back to the other side of the lake, and yes, you've guessed it, at the lakeside a massive crowd gathered all round him. [22] Now Jairus, who was some important geezer from the synagogue (the building that Jews worship in, just like Christians worship in a church, innit?) arrived and when he saw Jesus, he threw himself dahn at his plates, [23] and started begging. 'My little bottle is very Tom-and-Dick. Please come and lay your Ramsgates on her, so that she'll get better and live!' [24] Jesus started to walk with Jairus to his Mickey. There were loads of people everywhere, and Jesus was getting squashed in from every side.

[25] Now there was a woman who'd had terrible problems with losing blood; this had gone on for twelve years. [26] She had seen loads of doctors, and had spent all her bread, but she just kept getting worse and worse. [27] She'd heard about this Jesus geezer, so she followed him in the crowd, [28] saying to herself, 'If I can just touch 'is weasel, I'll get well.'

[29] Well, she touches 'is weasel, and would you Adam-and-Eve it, her bleeding stopped just like that; and she had that feeling

inside that her medical problems had gone. ³⁰ At this point, Jesus suddenly felt that some power had left him, and so 'e turned round and said, 'Who touched me weasel?' ³¹ His disciples looked at him as if 'e were daft and said, 'Oi, Guv. There's bloomin' millions of people around you, so why are you asking who touched your weasel?' ³² Jesus just carried on looking around. ³³ The woman knew what had happened to her, and so she came up to Jesus and knelt at his plates. The poor girl was terrified, so she told him the truth, not a single porky. ³⁴ Jesus said to her, 'Me bottle, it is your faith that has made you well. Now go in peace. Your troubles are over.'

³⁵ As Jesus was saying all this, some geezers came from Jairus' house, and they said to him, 'Your bottle 'as died. No need to bother the Teacher any more.' ³⁶ Jesus didn't pay a blind bit of notice to them, and he said to the ruler of the synagogue, 'Don't worry mate, just believe.' ³⁷ Jesus didn't let anyone continue with him except for Peter and James and his brother John. ³⁸ They got to Jairus' Mickey, and there was a load of confusion, people 'aving a real old snoop-and-pry. ³⁹ Jesus went in and said, 'What's the problem? Why all this snoop and prying? This little girl ain't brown bread, she's just 'aving a kip!' ⁴⁰ They all laughed at him. So 'e chucked them all out, took the girl's mum and dad, and 'is three disciples, and went into the room where the young girl was lying. ⁴¹ He took her by the German and said to her, '*Talitha, Koum,*' and that means, 'Oi, little girl, get up!' ⁴² Well, blimey! She got up at once and started walking around. (This girl, by the way, was twelve years old.) Not surprising, everyone who saw this was bloomin' shocked. ⁴³ Jesus told them all that they weren't to tell no one about this. He then said, 'Give the poor girl something to eat.'

Jesus has a rough time at Nazareth

(MATTHEW 13:53–58; LUKE 4:16–30)

6 Jesus left that place and went back to his own home town. His disciples tagged along behind. ² On the ol' Sabbath he started to teach in the synagogue. There was quite a crowd there. When they all heard him teaching away as 'e did, they were all quite amazed. 'How does this geezer know all this?' they wondered. 'How does 'e know about all these things? How on earth does 'e do all these miracles? ³ He's just a simple woodworker, ain't 'e, the son of Mary, and the brother of James, Joseph, Judas and Simon? Don't his skin-and-blisters live 'ere as well?' All the people started 'aving a go at him. ⁴ Jesus said to all of them, 'A prophet is respected all over the place, but never in his own neck of the woods, and by his relatives and his family.' ⁵ Jesus weren't able to do any of his miracles there, but he did place his hands on a few people who were feeling a little Tom-and-Dick, and he healed them. ⁶ Jesus was quite a bit shocked 'cos the people had no faith.

Jesus gives 'is twelve disciples a little job to do
(MATTHEW 10:5–15; LUKE 9:1–6)

Jesus then had a little ball around all the villages there, teaching the people as 'e normally did. ⁷ He then called the twelve disciples together, and 'e sent them all out on a mission, two by two. Jesus gave his chinas power over them nasty evil spirits, ⁸ an' 'e said to them, 'Don't take nothing with you on your journey except a stick. Don't take any Uncle Fred, no bag to go begging with, and no bees in your pocket. ⁹ You're to wear sandals, and you ain't to carry an extra Uncle Bert.' ¹⁰ Jesus also went on to say, 'When people welcome you, stay in the same Mickey until you are ready to leave there. ¹¹ If you come to some dodgy town where people don't welcome you, or won't even listen to you, just leave, and shake the dust off your plates. That'll teach them, and will be a nice little warning to them!'

¹² So, Jesus' twelve mates went out and starting preaching away, telling people that they should turn away from their sins. ¹³ They had a good scrap with loads of demons and drove them all away. They rubbed some olive oil on people who were a little bit Tom, and they got better.

The death of John the Bappy (Baptist)

(MATTHEW 14:1–12; LUKE 9:7–9)

[14] Now King Herod, a nasty piece of work, got to hear about all this. This geezer Jesus' reputation was spreading everywhere. Some people were even saying, 'John the Bappy has come back to life! That's why 'e's got all this power to do all these miracles and that.' [15] Other people were saying, 'He's Elijah.' Other people were saying, 'He's a prophet, like one of those prophets from ages ago.'

[16] When Herod heard it, 'e said, 'He's bloomin' John the Bappy! I had 'is loaf cut off, but he has obviously come back to life!' [17] It was Herod who had John arrested, and had him chucked into prison, all chained up. Herod did this because of his woman—Herodias 'er name was. He'd married her even though she was the trouble of his brother, Philip. [18] John the Bappy kept on tellin' ol' Herod, 'It's a bloomin' disgrace that you're married to your brother's trouble-and-strife!' [19] Because of this, Herodias really hated John the Bappy, and she wanted to kill him, but she couldn't, 'cos of Herod. [20] Herod was really scared of John 'cos 'e knew that John was a good and holy geezer. Herod kept him safe. He used to like to listen to him, even though it made him feel a bit disturbed every time he heard him. [21] However, Herodias eventually got her chance to do away with John once and for all. It was on Herod's birthday, and 'e had a massive party for all the top people, like government officials, the military, and some of the most important people in Galilee. Anybody who was anybody was there! [22] The bottle of Herodias came in and did a little dance. Herod loved it, and so did all his guests. So the king said to her, 'What do you fancy? You can have whatever you want. I'll even give you 'alf me kingdom if you want!' [24] The girl went out and said to her mum, 'What shall I ask for?'

'The loaf of John the Bappy,' she answered. [25] The girl went straight back to the king and said, 'I want the loaf of John the Bappy here and now on a dish!' [26] The king was gutted. He couldn't say no 'cos he'd made these promises in front of all 'is guests. [27] So he told one of 'is guards to go and bring John's loaf. The guard went and chopped off his loaf. [28] He then brought it on a dish and gave it to the girl, and she gave it to 'er finger-and-thumb. [29] When John's followers had heard about this, they arrived to collect his body, and then they buried it.

Jesus feeds five thousand geezers

(MATTHEW 14:13–21; LUKE 9:10–17; JOHN 6:1–14)

[30] Jesus' chinas met up with 'im, and they told him all they'd done, and all about their preaching. [31] There were so many people about that Jesus and his little group of apostles didn't even have time for a bite to eat. So 'e said to 'em, 'Oi, fellas, let's pop off on our Jack for a while and have a little rest and a kip.' [32] So they got into a nanny and headed off to a quiet place.

[33] Loads of people saw them leaving—people from all the different towns, who ran like the clappers by land, and arrived at the same place Jesus was headed for. But they arrived before Jesus and his mates did. [34] So when Jesus got out of the old nanny, 'e saw this bloomin' huge crowd, and he felt sorry for them, 'cos they were like little lost sheep without a shepherd. Jesus started to teach them loads of things. [35] Now time was getting on, and a little alligator his disciples came up to him and said, 'It's getting a little bit late, boss, and this is a really lonely place. [36] We think we should send all these people to some of the farms and villages dahn the old frog so that they can buy some nosh to eat.'

[37] 'Why don't you give 'em something to eat?' Jesus asked.

'Now hang on, boss,' they said. 'Are we gonna have to spend two hundred silver coins on Uncle Fred in order to feed this lot?'

[38] Jesus asked, 'How much grub 'ave you got? Go an' 'ave a butcher's.' After they'd 'ad a look, they came back and told 'im, 'We've got five loaves of Uncle Fred and two Lilian Gish.'

[39] Jesus then told his disciples to ask all the people to get into groups and sit dahn on the grass. [40] Everyone sat dahn in rows, some groups with about fifty people in, and some with a hundred. [41] Jesus then took the Uncle Fred and the Lilian Gish, 'e looked up to heaven and said 'Ta' to God. He then broke the Uncle Fred into bits, gave it all to his disciples, and told them to give some food to

everyone. He also broke the Lilian Gish into bits and told his mates to pass it round. [42] Now, would you Adam-and-Eve it, everyone 'ad enough to eat! [43] Even more surprising was that there was loads of nosh left—enough to fill up twelve baskets! [44] The number of geezers who were fed was about five thousand.

Jesus walks on the bloomin' fisherman's!
(MATTHEW 14:22–33; JOHN 6:15–21)

[45] Jesus then told his little gang to get straight into the nanny and go on to a place called Bethsaida, which was on the other side of the lake. Meanwhile, Jesus sent all the people away. [46] When he'd said 'Ta-ta' to all the people, 'e went to a Jack to 'ave a little pray. [47] When evening came along, as it does, the nanny was in the middle of the lake. Jesus, meanwhile, was on his Tod on the land. [48] Now 'e could see that his disciples were 'aving a little problem rowing against the wind. They were really straining at the oars. Some time between three and six o'clock in the morning Jesus came to them, walking on the bloomin' fisherman's! He was gonna just walk on by them, [49] but his mates saw 'im walking on the fisherman's. 'Blimey! It's a ghost!' they all thought, and they screamed, 'Agghhhh!' [50] They were scared stiff when they saw him.

Jesus spoke to them straight away. 'Calm dahn, boys. Have a little courage. It's only me. Don't be scared!' [51] He then got into the old boat with them, and the wind died dahn. The disciples were totally amazed. Who can blame 'em! [52] The disciples were still amazed at the feeding of the five thousand, because they hadn't really understood the meaning of what had gone on. Their poor little minds just couldn't take it all in.

Jesus heals the Tom-and-Dick in Gennesaret
(MATTHEW 14:34–36)

[53] They all eventually crossed the lake and came to land at a place called Gennesaret. They tied up the nanny. [54] As they left the nanny,

people immediately recognized Jesus. ⁵⁵ They ran from over the whole area to try and see him, and wherever he was, all the Tom-and-Dick were brought to 'im lying on their dogs. ⁵⁶ In all the villages, towns and farms that Jesus visited, all the Tom-and-Dick folk were brought to him, to the marketplaces, and they begged him to let them at least touch the edge of 'is weasel; and all those who touched it got better.

The teaching of the geezers from the past—the ancestors
(MATTHEW 15:1–9)

7 Some Pharisees and some teachers of the Law (the heavy mob!) who had travelled dahn from Jerusalem gathered round Jesus. ² They happened to spot that some of his disciples were eating their grub with Germans that hadn't been cleaned in a special ritual. The Pharisees had special rules about how to wash your Germans, and the disciples hadn't done this. ³ (As far as the Pharisees were concerned, as well as the Jews in general, they all followed the teaching which they got from their ancestors. For example, you're not to eat anything unless you wash your Germans in the proper way; ⁴ and you're not to eat anything that comes from the market unless you wash it first. There were loads of other rules you had to follow as well, like how you're supposed to wash cups, pots and dishes.)

⁵ As you can guess, the Pharisees and teachers of the Law were not too happy with Jesus, and so they asked 'im, 'How is it, mate, that your disciples don't follow the proper teaching handed dahn by our ancestors, and sit there eating with ritually dirty German Bands?'

⁶ Jesus said, 'The prophet Isaiah was right about you lot! You're all bloomin' hypocrites, just like he wrote: "These people, says God, they use all these fancy dicky birds to praise and honour me, but their stop-and-start isn't in it. ⁷ There's no point them worshipping me, because they teach all these man-made rules as though they were bloomin' God's laws!" ⁸ 'You seem to have got rid of God's

command, and only bother about the teachings of men.' ⁹ And Jesus carried on, 'You lot have got a clever old way of forgetting about God's law just so's you can keep your own teaching. ¹⁰ Moses himself said, "Respect your mum and dad," and, "Whoever cusses his mum or dad is to be put to death." ¹¹ But you lot seem to teach that if someone has something he *could* use to help 'is mum or dad, but says instead, "This is Corban" (meaning it belongs to God), ¹² then he's excused from helping his mum or dad. ¹³ By allowing this, you're cancelling out the word of God. And there's loads of other things that you lot are doing like that.'

The sort of things that make a person dirty
(MATTHEW 15:10–20)

¹⁴ Jesus then called out to the crowd, 'Oi, listen up, and try to understand me. ¹⁵⁻¹⁶ There's nothin' that goes into you from the outside that can make you dirty in a religious way. What makes you dirty is what comes out of ya!'

¹⁷ When Jesus had left the crowd and went into the Mickey, his disciples wanted to know what it was that he had been talking about. ¹⁸ 'Blimey! You're just as daft as the rest,' Jesus said to 'em. 'Don't you bloomin' understand anything? What goes into a person from the outside can't really make you dirty ¹⁹ because it don't go into your stop-and-start but into your Aunty Nellie and later it all goes out of the body again.' (By saying this, Jesus is basically saying that all foods are OK to be eaten.) ²⁰ Jesus then went on to say, 'It's what comes out of people that makes them dirty. ²¹ Out of someone's stop-and-start come all those nasty ideas which can lead you to do dodgy things like become a tea leaf, kill people, sleep around, cheating on your husbands and wives (called adultery), ²² be greedy, and all sorts of other nasty things— telling porkies, indecency, being jealous, slagging people off, pride. ²³ All these terrible things come from inside a person and make that person dirty.'

A lady's faith

(MATTHEW 15:21–28)

24 Jesus then left there and went to some area near the city of Tyre. He went into a Mickey, and he didn't want anyone to know that 'e was there, but as bloomin' usual, 'e couldn't stay hidden. 25 Some lady, whose little ribbon had an evil spirit in her, heard about this Jesus geezer, and came to him as soon as possible, and she fell at his plates. 26 This woman was a Gentile (she weren't a Jew), and she was born in the area of Phoenicia in Syria. She begged and begged Jesus to give the demon a good slap and drive it out of 'er daughter. 27 But Jesus said, 'First we've gotta feed the saucepans. It ain't right to take the saucepans' food and chuck it to the dogs.' 28 'But please, sir,' she said, 'even the dogs under the Cain-and-Abel eat the saucepans' leftovers!' 29 Jesus said, 'Because of that answer, go back to your Mickey, and you'll find that the demon has gone out of your little ribbon!' 30 She went home and, strike-a-light, she found her daughter lying on the Uncle Ned, and the demon had vanished!

Jesus heals a Mutt-and-Jeff geezer
who couldn't rabbit either

31 Jesus left this area around Tyre and travelled through Sidon to Lake Galilee, passing by the area of the Ten Towns. 32 Some geezer was brought to him who was Mutt-and-Jeff and who could hardly rabbit. The people who brought this geezer to Jesus begged him to place his Germans on 'im and heal 'im. 33 Jesus went off alone with the Mutt-and-Jeff geezer, well away from the crowd, and 'e put 'is fingers in the geezer's ears, spat, and then touched his tongue. 34 Jesus then looked up to heaven, groaned, and said to the geezer, 'Ephphatha' (Jesus' own language which means, 'Open up!').

35 Straight away the geezer could hear, and 'e started rabbiting on without any hassle. 36 Jesus told everybody that they mustn't tell anyone what they'd seen that day; but as bloomin' usual, the more 'e told them not to, the more they rabbited on about the miracle. 37 Everyone who 'eard about it was bloomin' amazed. 'This Jesus

does everything so well!' they shouted. 'He even helps the Mutt-and-Jeff to hear and the dumb to rabbit!'

This time Jesus feeds four thousand people
(MATTHEW 15:32–39)

8 Not long afterwards, another massive crowd turned up. When they all had nothing left to nosh, Jesus called 'is disciples and said, ² 'I feel sorry for this lot, 'cos they've been with me for three days and now they're bloomin' Hank Marvin. They've got nothing to eat. ³ I can't send them all home now without giving them some food, 'cos they'll all bloomin' faint; some of 'em live miles away!' ⁴ The disciples, looking very puzzled, asked, 'Where on earth in this bloomin' desert are we supposed to find enough grub to feed this lot?' ⁵ 'How much Uncle Fred 'ave you got?' Jesus asked. 'Seven loaves,' they said. ⁶ Jesus asked all the people to sit dahn on the safe. He took the seven loaves of Uncle Fred, said 'Ta' to God, broke it all, and 'e gave it to 'is disciples to dish out to the crowd; and that's just what they did. ⁷ They also had some small Lilian. Jesus said 'Ta' for these, and had his disciples dish them out as well. ⁸⁻⁹ Everybody had a good old nosh; there were at least four thousand people there. At the end, the disciples collected up seven baskets of leftover food. Jesus was now able to send the people away ¹⁰ and he got straight into a nanny with his chinas and went on to the district of Dalmanutha.

Those bloomin' Pharisees want a miracle
(MATTHEW 16:1–4)

¹¹ Some of those Pharisees came to see Jesus, and they had a right ol' go at him. They were trying to catch 'im out, so they asked 'im to do a miracle to prove that God was on 'is side. ¹² Jesus, obviously a bit fed up with them, just groaned and said, 'Why do this lot today ask for a miracle? No way! I'm not givin' any bloomin' proof to this lot!' ¹³ He left them, got back in the old nanny, and set off for the other side of the lake.

Jesus goes on about the yeast of the Pharisees and of Herod

(MATTHEW 16:5–12)

14 Now the silly ol' disciples had forgotten to bring enough Uncle Fred with them, and they only had one loaf between them in the nanny. 15 'You'd better take care,' Jesus suddenly warned them. 'You've gotta be on your guard against the yeast of the Pharisees and the yeast of Herod.' 16 The disciples didn't have a bloomin' clue what 'e was on about. They said, 'Is 'e saying this just 'cos we ain't got any Uncle Fred?' 17 Jesus knew exactly what they were rabbiting on about, so 'e asked 'em, 'Why are you rabbiting on about not 'aving any Uncle Fred? Haven't you got a clue what I'm going on about? Are you that Piccadilly? 18 You've got mince pies; can't you bloomin' see? You've got ears; can't you bloomin' hear? Can't you lot remember 19 when I broke them five loaves of Uncle Fred for those five thousand people? How many bloomin' baskets full of leftover grub did you end up with?' 'Twelve,' they said. 20 'And when I broke those seven loaves for them four thousand people,' asked Jesus, 'how many baskets full of nosh did we have then?' 'Seven,' they said. 21 'And you still have no bloomin' idea?' he asked them.

Jesus heals a blind geezer at Bethsaida

22 They all ended up at a place called Bethsaida. Some people turned up and they had with them a geezer who was as blind as a bat. They begged Jesus to touch this blind geezer and heal him. 23 Jesus took the blind geezer's German and led him out of the village. Jesus spat on the geezer's mince pies (charming!), and placed 'is Germans on him and asked 'im, 'What can you see, mate?' 24 The geezer looked up and said, 'Blimey. I can see people, but they all look like a load of trees walking around.' 25 Jesus then placed his Germans on the geezer's mince pies again. This time the geezer had a real good butcher's, and his eyesight came back. He could see everything as right as rain! 26 Jesus sent the geezer home, but told him not to go back to the village.

Peter has a good idea about who this Jesus geezer really is

(MATTHEW 16:13–20; LUKE 9:18–21)

27 Jesus and his little gang went off to the villages near Caesarea Philippi. As they were plodding along Jesus asked them, 'Oi, fellas. What do all these people round 'ere think about me? Who do you reckon they think I am?'

28 'Some people reckon you're John the Bappy,' they answered. 'Some other people reckon you're that great prophet geezer Elijah, or one of the other great prophets.'

29 'And what about you lot; who do you really think I am?'

Peter spoke up, 'You, mate, are the guv'nor—the Messiah.'

30 Jesus then said, 'Now listen up. Make sure you don't tell no one about me.'

Jesus tells his mates that he's gonna have to be slapped around a bit and then kick the bucket

(MATTHEW 16:21–28; LUKE 9:22–27)

31 Jesus then started to teach his mates a thing or two. 'I am the currant of Man and I'm gonna have to suffer a fair old bit. The important religious people, the elders, the chief priests and teachers of the Law are all gonna cause me a load of grief, and they're gonna get me killed. The currant of Man is gonna have to kick the bucket, but three days later 'e will come back to life again.' 32 Jesus told them all this as simply as 'e could. But Peter got 'imself in a right ol' two-and-eight, and started to 'ave a go at Jesus about all the death and suffering stuff. 33 But Jesus turned round, 'ad a butcher's at all his disciples, and then 'e really 'ad a go at Peter. 'Clear off Satan,' 'e screamed at Peter. 'What's goin' on in your loaf? Your thoughts don't come from God. You're just thinking like any old geezer!'

34 Then Jesus got his mates and all the crowd together, and 'e said to them, 'If any of you lot wanna come with me, then you're gonna have to stop thinking about yourselves. You're gonna have to be prepared for some hassle. You're gonna have to carry your own cross, and then follow me. 35 Because listen 'ere, if you wanna save

your own fork, you're gonna have to bloomin' lose it; and whoever loses his fork for me and for the good ol' gospel, will save it. [36] What's the point of winning the whole bloomin' world and yet lose your fork? There's no point. You'd be Piccadilly! [37] There ain't nothing you can give to get your fork back. [38] If anyone feels a little embarrassed and ashamed about me, an' all me teaching and that, in this bloomin' awful and godless lemon, then the currant of Man will be bloomin' ashamed of that person when 'e comes in the wonderful glory of 'is Father with the holy angels.'

9 He then carried on saying, 'Listen up, you lot. Some of you 'ere ain't gonna die until you've 'ad a good ol' butcher's at the kingdom of God come in real style and power.'

Blimey, here's a big word… the Transfiguration
(MATTHEW 17:1–13; LUKE 9:28–36)

[2] Six days later Jesus took with 'im Peter, James and John, and they went up a bloomin' high mountain. They were all on their Tod. As the disciples were wondering what was goin' on, Jesus suddenly started to change; [3] all his these-and-those became shining white; and not even your top bloomin' washing powder could get them this white! [4] All of a sudden, the three disciples saw Elijah (an important prophet geezer in the Old Testament) and Moses (yeah, Moses—the parting of the Red Sea geezer!) rabbiting away with Jesus. [5] Peter then said to Jesus, 'It's bloomin' great that we're all 'ere together! What we can do is make three tents, one for you, Guv, one for Moses and one for Elijah.' [6] Peter and the others were so bloomin' scared that they didn't really know what to say.

[7] All of a sudden it became quite cloudy, and Jesus, Moses and Elijah were covered in the cloud's shadow. And an Hobson's came from the cloud, 'This is my own dear currant; listen to what 'e 'as to say!' [8] The disciples 'ad a quick butcher's around, but couldn't see anyone else; it was only Jesus who was with them. [9] As they came dahn the old mountain, Jesus told 'em quite strictly, 'Now don't you dare tell anyone about what you've seen today, not until

the currant of Man has come back to fork.' [10] The disciples did as they were told, but they started rabbiting to each other. 'What on earth does Jesus mean about all this rising from the dead?' [11] They asked Jesus, 'Why do all the teachers of the Law and that lot say that Elijah has to come first?' [12] Jesus explained, 'Elijah is coming first to get everything ready, innit? But why do the holy writings say that the currant of Man will be slapped about and rejected? [13] Now listen 'ere. Elijah has already come, and all the people treated 'im like dirt, as the holy writings say about 'im.'

Jesus heals a boy who has one of those nasty evil spirits in 'im

(MATTHEW 17:14–21; LUKE 9:37–43A)

[14] When they got back from the mountain, they got together with the rest of the gang, who had been surrounded by a bloomin' large crowd. They was 'aving a righ' ol' argument, and some of those arguing were teachers of the Law. [15] As soon as the people saw Jesus, they were right surprised, and they ran up to 'im and said, 'Hello.' [16] Jesus then asked 'is disciples, 'What are you lot in such a two-and-eight for? What's all the arguing about?'

[17] Some geezer in the crowd answered, 'Guv, I brought my currant to you, 'cos 'e's got a nasty little evil spirit in 'im and 'e can't ball. [18] When the bloomin' spirit attacks 'im, 'e gets thrown to the safe, and 'e starts foaming at the north, grinding 'is bloomin' Hampsteads, an' 'e goes stiff all over. I asked your disciples to sort out this bloomin' spirit, but they can't.'

[19] Jesus said to 'em, 'How is it that you lot don't believe anything? How long do I have to bloomin' stay with you? How much longer do I have to put up with all this cherry? Bring the boy to me!' [20] They brought the little 'un to Jesus. As soon as the dodgy old spirit saw Jesus, it threw the poor boy into a fit. He was in a right old two-and-eight. He fell on to the safe and 'e was rolling around and foaming at the north. [21] 'How long as 'e been like this?' Jesus asked the dad.

'Since 'e was a little 'un,' he replied. 22 'There's been loads of times that the evil spirit 'as tried to kill 'im by throwing 'im in Jeremiah and into the fisherman's. Please help us if you can, Guv!'

23 'Yeah, all right,' said Jesus. 'But what's this about "if you can"? Everything is possible for the person who 'as faith.'

24 The dad then cried out, 'I do 'ave faith, Guv, but just not enough. Please 'elp me have more!'

25 Jesus could see that the crowd was getting closer and closer, so 'e said to the spirit, 'Now listen 'ere, you Mutt-and-Jeff spirit. I order you to come out of the boy and never come back, do you 'ear me?' 26 The spirit screamed; the boy was thrown into a terrible old fit, and then the spirit left 'im. The boy didn't move. He looked like a stiff. 'He's dead, innit?' everyone said. 27 But Jesus took the boy by 'is German and helped 'im get up, and 'e stood up.

28 Afterwards Jesus went inside, and his disciples asked 'im, 'Why on earth couldn't we get rid of that evil spirit?'

29 'Only prayer can get rid of this sort of spirit,' 'e said. 'Nothing else works with this sneaky kind of demon!'

Yet again, Jesus goes on about 'is death

(MATTHEW 17:22–23; LUKE 9:43B–45)

30 Jesus and 'is mates left that place, and they travelled on through Galilee. Jesus wanted no one to know where 'e was 31 'cos 'e was teaching 'is disciples. Jesus said to them, 'The currant of Man is gonna be given over to some men who are gonna do away with him, and three days later 'e is gonna rise to fork.' 32 Unfortunately, his disciples didn't have a bloomin' clue what 'e was on about, and they didn't dare ask 'im.

Who's the greatest?

(MATTHEW 18:1–5; LUKE 9:46–48)

33 They eventually arrived at Capernaum, and when they went indoors Jesus asked 'is disciples, 'What were you lot arguing about

on the frog?' [34] They didn't answer 'im because out on the frog they had been 'aving an argument about who was the greatest. [35] Jesus then sat dahn with 'is twelve mates and said to 'em, 'Now listen up. Whoever wants to be first must put 'imself last and be everybody's servant.' [36] He then took a kiddie and made 'im stand in front of them. He put his chalks around him and said to 'em, [37] 'Whoever welcomes one of these saucepans in my name, welcomes me; and whoever welcomes me, don't only welcome me but also the one who sent me, innit?'

Whoever ain't against us is bloomin' well for us
(LUKE 9:49–50)

[38] John said to Jesus, 'Guv, we saw some geezer who was driving out demons in your name, and we told 'im to knock it on the 'ead, to stop it, because 'e weren't one of us.'

[39] 'Don't try to stop 'im,' Jesus said. ''Cos no one who does miracles in my name will be able soon after, like, to say nasty and evil things about me. [40] 'Cos whoever ain't against us is bloomin' for us. [41] I can tell you now, anyone who gives you a tiddly of fisherman's 'cos you belong to me will definitely get a reward.'

Being tempted to sin
(MATTHEW 18:6–9; LUKE 17:1–2)

[42] 'Now listen 'ere. If anyone makes one of these little saucepans stop believing in me, I think it would be better for him to have a bloomin' big millstone tied round his bushel and be thrown into the bloomin' coffee. [43–44] So, if ya German causes you to stop believing in me, chop the bloomin' thing off! It's gonna be better for you to enter fork with one German than to keep both Germans and end up in hell, the Jeremiah that never goes out. [45–46] Same as if ya foot makes ya lose your faith, then chop it off! It's better for you to enter fork without a foot than to keep both ya plates and be thrown into hell. [47] And if ya mince causes you to lose ya faith, poke the thing

out. It's better for you to enter God's kingdom with only one mince than to keep both minces and be thrown into hell. [48] In that awful place the worms that eat them never die, and the Jeremiah never goes out. [49] Everyone is gonna be made pure by Jeremiah. [50] Salt is wonderful; but we all know that if it loses its saltiness, how can it ever be made salty again? You've gotta have the good old salt of friendship among yourselves. You've gotta live in peace with each other.'

What does the Guv'nor have to say about divorce?
(MATTHEW 19:1–12; LUKE 16:18)

10 Jesus then left there and went on to Judea, and 'e crossed the River Jordan. As usual, loads of people came to see 'im, and he taught them, like 'e always did. [2] Then, some Pharisees came to 'im and they were a little bit sneaky and tried to trap him. 'Oi you, Jesus geezer,' they said. 'Does our Law allow a geezer to get divorced from 'is trouble?' [3] Jesus answered their question with a question of his own—'e was good at doing that! 'What law did Moses give you?' Jesus asked. [4] They answered, 'Moses gave permission for a geezer to write a divorce notice, and to simply send 'is trouble away.' [5] Jesus said to 'em, 'The reason why Moses wrote this law for you is because you lot are so bloomin' hard to teach. [6] I can tell you this, in the very beginning, when everything was created, "God made them a geezer and a lady," just like it says in our holy writings. [7] "And for this reason a geezer will leave 'is mum and dad and join with 'is trouble, [8] and both of them will become one." So they ain't two any more, but one. [9] Therefore, what God has joined together, no one can split up.' [10] When they went back inside the old Mickey, the disciples wanted to know a little more about all this. [11] Jesus said to 'em, 'A geezer who divorces 'is trouble and marries another woman commits adultery against 'is trouble. [12] This also applies the other way round. If a woman divorces 'er 'usband and marries some other geezer, she is committing adultery.'

Jesus blesses all the little saucepans

(MATTHEW 19:13–15; LUKE 18:15–17)

13 Some people brought some saucepans to Jesus for him to place his Ramsgates on 'em, but the disciples got into a right old two-and-eight and shouted at the people. 14 When the guv'nor saw this, 'e was a little bit narked, and 'e said to 'is disciples, 'Let all the little saucepans come to me; don't stop 'em, because God's kingdom belongs to this lot. 15 Let me tell you now, unless you can receive the kingdom of God like one of these little kiddies, you'll never enter the kingdom.' 16 He then took the children in 'is chalks, placed 'is Germans on each one of them, and blessed them.

The rich geezer

(MATTHEW 19:16–30; LUKE 18:18–30)

17 Jesus was about to get going when some geezer ran up to 'im, knelt dahn before him, and then asked him, 'Oi, Guv, what have I got to do to live for ever, and have eternal life? Please tell me, Good Teacher.'

18 'Why are you calling me good?' Jesus asked him. 'Only God is good. 19 You must know all the commandments: "Don't murder; don't sleep with anyone else's woman or man; don't become a tea leaf and steal; don't go around accusing people wrongly; don't cheat; make sure you respect your mum and your old man."' 20 'Teacher,' the geezer said, 'ever since I was a young 'un, I've always obeyed these commandments.' 21 Jesus looked straight at this geezer in a real loving sort of way, and 'e said to 'im, 'You've only got to do one thing. Go and sell everything you own and then give all the bread to the on-the-floor, you'll then have loads of riches in heaven. Then when you've done all that, come and follow me.' 22 When the geezer heard this, you should've seen 'is boat; 'e looked really fed up. He ball-of-chalked off feeling really sad, 'cos 'e was so bloomin' rich! 23 Jesus 'ad a good butcher's at his disciples and said to them, 'Do you realize how bloomin' difficult it's gonna be for rich people to get into God's kingdom?' 24 The disciples were right

shocked when Jesus said this, and Jesus went on to say, 'Listen 'ere. It's gonna be bloomin' hard to enter the kingdom of God! ²⁵ Do you realize that it is much harder for a rich person to enter the kingdom of God than it is for a blinkin' camel to go through the mince of a needle.' ²⁶ And now the disciples were totally amazed, and they started to say to each other, 'Well, who on earth can get into the kingdom?' ²⁷ Jesus had a good butcher's at them and said, 'It may be totally impossible for people, but it ain't impossible for God, 'cos God can do anything.'

²⁸ Peter then said, 'But, Guv, we've left everything and we're following you.'

²⁹ 'I know,' said Jesus, 'and let me tell you this; anyone who leaves 'ome or brothers or skins or mum and dad or saucepans or fields for me and for the good ol' gospel ³⁰ will receive much more now. They'll receive a hundred times more Mickeys, brothers, skins, mums, saucepans and fields; but also a load of hassle and persecutions; but in the next ol' age, they'll receive eternal fork. ³¹ Loads of people who think they're first at the moment will actually be last, and loads of people who are now last will actually be first.'

This is now the third time that Jesus talks about 'is death

(MATTHEW 20:17–19; LUKE 18:31–34)

³² Jesus and 'is little gang were now on the frog going up to Jerusalem. Jesus was ball-of-chalking ahead of 'em, and they were actually quite amazed, and the people who were tagging on behind were afraid. (They was all bloomin' amazed and afraid, 'cos Jesus was on 'is way to Jerusalem where 'e said 'e was gonna get killed.) As he'd done before, Jesus took the twelve disciples to one side and started telling them what was gonna happen to 'im. ³³ 'Now listen up,' he said. 'We're now going up to Jerusalem where the currant of Man is gonna be given over to the chief priests and the teachers of the Law. They're gonna have a real go at 'im and then they'll want to do away with him. They'll condemn him to death, and then

they'll give 'im to the Gentiles (non-Jews, Romans) [34] and they'll make fun of 'im, they'll spit on 'im, whip him, and then they'll kill him; but three days later he'll come to life again.'

James and John ask Jesus for a little favour
(MATTHEW 20:20–28)

[35] James and John, who were currants of Zebedee, came up to Jesus, and they asked him, 'Guv, there's something we'd like you to do for us.'

[36] 'Yeah. What is it?' Jesus asked them.

[37] They said, 'When you eventually sit on your throne in your wonderful kingdom—'cos you're the guv'nor—we'd like to be able to sit with you, one on your right and one on your left.'

[38] 'Do you two really know what you're asking for?' Jesus said to them. 'Will you be able to tiddly the terrible cup of suffering that I must tiddly? Will you be able to be baptized in the way that I must be baptized?'

[39] 'Yep,' they answered.

Jesus said to 'em, 'You definitely will tiddly the cup I must tiddly and also be baptized in the way that I must be baptized. [40] But listen here, fellas; I really don't have the right to choose who's gonna sit at me Isle and me left. It's God who prepares all the places. It's up to 'im who goes where.' [41] When the other ten disciples heard about all this, they got into a right ol' two-and-eight, and were bloomin' angry with James and John. [42] So Jesus got them all together and said, 'You all know that the geezers who are the leaders of all the heathen and unbelievers have power over them, and these leaders have complete authority. [43] But this isn't how it is with you lot. If one of you wants to be great, then you've gotta be the servant of the rest; [44] and if one of you wants to be first, 'e's gotta be the slave to everyone else. [45] 'Cos even the currant of Man didn't come here to be served—'e came to serve others and to give his fork to save people and bring 'em back to God.'

Jesus heals a blind geezer called Bartimaeus

(MATTHEW 20:29–34; LUKE 18:35–43)

⁴⁶ Jesus and 'is mates arrived in Jericho, and as Jesus was leaving with them and a large crowd, a blind geezer—a beggar called Bartimaeus, currant of Timaeus—was sitting by the frog. ⁴⁷ When 'e heard that it was this Jesus geezer from Nazareth, 'e started to shout, 'Oi! Jesus! Currant of David! Please take pity on me!' ⁴⁸ Many of the people there had a right old go at the blind geezer, and they told him to shut up. But 'e just started to shout even louder, 'Oi! Currant of David, take pity on me!' ⁴⁹ Jesus stopped and said, 'Call that geezer over here.' So they said to the blind geezer, 'Cheer up mate. Come on. He's calling you.' ⁵⁰ The geezer threw off his weasel, jumped up, and then came to Jesus. ⁵¹ 'What can I do for you then, mate?' Jesus asked him. 'Teacher,' the blind geezer answered, 'I wanna be able to see again.'

⁵² 'Off you go, mate,' Jesus said to him. 'Your faith has made you well.' The geezer was able to see again, and 'e followed Jesus on the frog.

Jesus enters Jerusalem in style

(MATTHEW 21:1–11; LUKE 19:28–40; JOHN 12:12–19)

11 As they got close to Jerusalem, near the towns of Bethphage and Bethany, they came to the Mount of Olives. (This place 'appens to be quite interesting. The geezer who was supposed to come and save everyone, who the Jews called the Messiah, was supposed to actually go to this place, the Mount of Olives. Jesus is the Messiah, and 'e goes to this place, also known as the Jack-and-Jill of oil. Messiah actually means 'Anointed One', anointed with oil. So, all these things are happening 'cos this Jesus geezer really is the currant of God, the Messiah.) Jesus sent two of his mates on ahead ² and 'e gave them these instructions: 'Go into the village you can see ahead of you, and when you get there, you'll see a colt tied up which ain't never been ridden. Untie it and bring it here. ³ If anyone asks you what you're doin', just tell them that the guv'nor needs it and he'll send it back as soon as possible.' ⁴ So they did as they were told,

and they found a colt out in the street, tied to the Rory of a Mickey. As they were untying it, ⁵ some people looking on said, 'Oi! What are you doin' with that animal?' ⁶ They answered just as Jesus had told them to, and they had no problems. ⁷ They brought the colt to Jesus, threw their weasels over the animal, and Jesus got on. ⁸ Loads of people spread their weasels on the frog, and loads of others cut branches in the fields and spread them on the frog. ⁹ The people in front and those behind started shouting, 'Praise God! God bless the geezer who comes in the name of the Lord! ¹⁰ God bless the coming kingdom of King David, our father! Praise God!' ¹¹ Jesus eventually entered Jerusalem, and 'e went into the Temple and 'ad a good butcher's at everything. It was quite late now, so 'e went out to Bethany with his twelve mates.

Jesus has a right old go at a fig tree!
(MATTHEW 21:18–19)

¹² The next day, as they were coming back from Bethany, Jesus was Hank Marvin. ¹³ In the distance 'e could see a fig tree and it was covered with leaves, so 'e went up to the tree to find some figs. When 'e got there, 'e saw that there were only leaves on the tree and no figs, 'cos it weren't the right time of year for figs. ¹⁴ Jesus said to the tree, 'No one is ever goin' to eat figs from you again!' (Charming!) His disciples heard him.

Jesus goes bananas in the Temple
(MATTHEW 21:12–17; LUKE 19:45–48; JOHN 2:13–22):

¹⁵ When they got to Jerusalem, Jesus went to the Temple, and 'e started going mad and chasing out all the people who were there buying and selling stuff. He turned over all the Cain-and-Abels belonging to the money-changers and those who were selling pigeons, ¹⁶ and 'e wouldn't let anyone carry anything through the Temple courtyards. ¹⁷ He then started to teach the people: 'Now listen. It's written in the Scriptures that God said, "My Temple will

be called a Mickey of prayer for the people of all nations." But you lot have turned it into a bloomin' hideout for tea leaves!' 18 All the important geezers, the chief priests and the teachers of the Law heard all this girls-and-boys, so they started to think of how they could do away with this Jesus geezer. They wanted 'im brown bread. They were all afraid of him, because the crowd seemed to love his teaching. They were all amazed. 19 In the evening, Jesus and 'is disciples left the city.

It's the fig tree again!
(MATTHEW 21:18–22)

20 Early next morning, as they ball-of-chalked along the frog, they saw that bloomin' fig tree again. It was completely brown bread all the way dahn to its roots. 21 Peter remembered what had happened and 'e said to Jesus, 'Oi, Guv. The fig tree you had a go at 'as died!'

22 Jesus said to them, 'Just have faith in God. 23 I'll tell you this—whoever tells this Jack to get up and throw itself in the coffee and doesn't doubt it in their stop, but really Adams that it's gonna happen, it will happen for them. 24 So listen up while I explain to you: When you pray and ask God for something, you've gotta really believe that you've received it, innit? And then you'll be given whatever you've asked for. 25–26 When you stand and pray, make sure you forgive anyone who you need to forgive, and then God in heaven will be able to forgive you for all the dodgy things that you've done wrong.'

The important geezers ask Jesus what gives 'im the right to do all the things he's doing
(MATTHEW 21:23–27; LUKE 20:1–8)

27 They arrived again in Jerusalem. As Jesus was 'aving a little ball through the Temple, the usual old gang, the chief priests, teachers of the Law and the elders came up to him and starting hassling him. 28 They asked him, 'What Isle-of-Wight do you have to go around

doing all this stuff? Who gave you this bloomin' right?' ²⁹ Jesus answered them, 'Let me ask you lot a question first, and if you can give me an answer, I'll tell you all what Isle I have to do all these things. ³⁰ Now tell me this, who gave John the Bappy the right to baptize: was it from God, or was it from man?' (Nice one, Jesus; let's see them get out of this one!) ³¹ They all started arguing among themselves: 'What on earth shall we say? If we tell 'im, "From God," he's gonna say, "Well why didn't you bloomin' well believe John?" ³² But if we tell 'im, "From man..."' Now they were really scared of the people, 'cos everyone was certain that John had been a prophet. ³³ So, the only answer they could give to Jesus was, 'We ain't got a clue!' Jesus then said to them, 'Well I ain't gonna tell you by what right I do all the things that I do.'

Story time: a parable about the tenants in the vineyard
(MATTHEW 21:33–46; LUKE 20:9–19)

12 Jesus then started to teach away again in parables. 'There was this geezer who planted a vineyard, and 'e put a great bloomin' fence around it, dug a hole to use for the winepress, to make the old rise-and-shine, and 'e built a watch-tower. He then rented out the vineyard to some tenants, and 'e went on a journey to another country. ² When the lemon came to gather in the grapes, he sent a slave along to the tenants to collect from them his share of the harvest. ³ But the bloomin' tenants grabbed hold of the slave, gave 'im a good kicking, and sent him back with nothing. ⁴ The owner then sent another bloomin' slave; he also got a good kicking and had his loaf slapped about. ⁵ The owner then sent another slave, and they actually killed this one. Loads of other slaves who were sent also got a good kicking, or were done away with. ⁶ The owner only had one more person left to send, and that was 'is own dear currant. So the owner sent his currant to the tenants. 'They're bound to show some respect to me old currant,' he said. ⁷ But those dodgy tenants said to each other, 'Oi. This is the owner's currant. Come on, let's give 'im a good kicking and do away with him, then his property will be ours!' ⁸ So they grabbed hold of the currant and bloomin' well killed him, and they threw his body out of the vineyard. ⁹ So, what's the owner gonna do now? I'll tell you what he's gonna do. He's gonna come and kill those men and give his vineyard to some other tenants. ¹⁰ You must have all read what it says in our holy writings? "The stone which all the brickies got rid off 'cos it was no good turned out to be the most bloomin' important stone of all. ¹¹ This was all done by the Lord, and what a bloomin' marvellous sight it is!"' ¹² All the Jewish leaders were now desperate to have Jesus nicked, because they knew for sure that this parable was told against them. (The tenants in this parable represented the Jewish leaders, ya see, and the currant in the parable represented Jesus. Clever, hey?) The Jewish leaders couldn't have 'im nicked there and then, 'cos they were afraid of the crowd, so they left 'im and pushed off.

Jesus gives a clever answer about paying taxes
(MATTHEW 22:15–22; LUKE 20:20–26)

¹³ Now some Pharisees and some members of Herod's gang were sent to try to trap Jesus by asking him some more daft questions. ¹⁴ They came up to 'im and said, 'Oi, Teacher, we know that everything you say is Irish, and that you don't worry about what people think, no matter who they are, rich, on the floor, or whatever. You teach people about what God really wants for us all. Can you please answer us this little question: Is it against our Law to pay taxes to that Roman Emperor geezer? ¹⁵ Do we have to pay our taxes or not?' Now Jesus wasn't Piccadilly; 'e knew they were trying to trap him, and 'e said, 'Why are you lot always trying to trap me? Bring me a silver coin and let me 'ave a butcher's at it.' ¹⁶ They brought 'im one, and 'e asked them, 'Whose boat and name are these?'

'The bloomin' Emperor's,' they answered.

¹⁷ Jesus then very cleverly said, 'Well then, pay the Emperor what belongs to 'im, and pay God what belongs to God.' (A bloomin' good answer!) They were all amazed at Jesus.

And now some more questions for Jesus, this time about rising from the dead

(MATTHEW 22:23–33; LUKE 20:27–40)

[18] Then some Sadducees (this bunch didn't believe in life after death), came up to Jesus and said to 'im, [19] 'Guv, Moses gave us this law: "If a geezer dies and leaves a trouble but no kids, that geezer's brother must marry the widow so that they can have kids who'll be considered the dead geezer's kids." [20] Now listen up, Guv. Once there were seven brothers, and the eldest one got himself cut-and-carried and 'e died without having any kids. [21] The second brother cut the woman, and 'e also died without 'aving any kids. Now the same thing happened to the third brother, [22] and then to all the rest; all seven of the brothers cut the woman and died without having any kids. [23] Now then, Jesus, when all the brown bread rise to life on the day of resurrection, whose trouble will she be? All seven of the geezers had married 'er.'

[24] 'Don't be so bloomin' Piccadilly,' Jesus answered them. 'You're so wrong! I'll tell you why, shall I? It's 'cos you don't understand our holy writings or God's power. [25] When the brown bread rise to fork, they're gonna be like all the angels in heaven, and won't get cut. [26] Now, about the brown bread being raised to fork: haven't you lot ever read in the rookery of Moses the famous little passage about the burning bush? It says there quite clearly that God said to Moses, "I am the God of Abraham, the God of Isaac, and the God of Jacob." [27] In other words, you daft lot, he's the God of the living, not the bloomin' brown bread. You lot are totally wrong!'

The really great commandment

(MATTHEW 22:34–40; LUKE 10:25–28)

[28] There was a teacher of the Law there who was listening to this big old discussion. He saw how Jesus gave a great answer back to the Sadducees, so 'e came up with a question of his own. 'Oi, Jesus! Which commandment would you say was the greatest of them all?'

[29] Jesus answered, 'This is the most important one: "Listen up,

Israel! The Lord our God is the only Lord. ³⁰ You are to turtle the Lord your God with all your stop, with all your soul, with all your mind, and with all your strength." ³¹ And this is the second most important commandment: "You are to turtle your neighbour as you turtle yourself." There is no other commandment as important as these two.' ³² The teacher geezer said to Jesus, 'Nice one, Guv. A good answer. It is Irish, just like you say, that only the Lord is God, and there ain't no other god but him. ³³ Also, that people must turtle God with all of their stop, mind and with all their strength, and they must turtle their neighbour as they turtle themselves. It's far more bloomin' important to follow and obey these two commandments than to offer up animals and other sacrifices to God.' ³⁴ Jesus was well impressed with 'is wise answer and so he told 'im, 'You're not far off from God's kingdom, mate.' After all this, no one dared ask Jesus any more questions.

Jesus explains a bit about the Messiah
(MATTHEW 22:41–46; LUKE 20:41–44)

³⁵ As Jesus was having a little teach in the Temple, 'e asked this question: 'How can all the teachers of the Law say that the Messiah will be a descendant of David? ³⁶ The Holy Spirit once caused David to say, "The Lord said to my Lord, 'Sit here at my right German till I put your enemies under your plates.'" ³⁷ Now listen, even David called him "Lord"; so how on earth can the Messiah be a bloomin' descendant of David? Use your loaf!'

Jesus warns people about these dodgy teachers of the Law
(MATTHEW 23:1–36; LUKE 20:45–47)

A large old crowd was happily listening to Jesus teaching away. ³⁸ As 'e was teaching them, he said, 'You'd better watch out for all these teachers of the Law, who ball-and-chalk around in their long robes and like to be greeted with respect in the marketplace, ³⁹ and they always have the bloomin' best seats reserved in the synagogues, and they always have the best places at all the feasts. [40] They don't give a bloomin' monkey's about the on-the-floor widows, and they pinch their homes, and then they make a bloomin' massive show by saying all their long meaningless prayers. It makes you feel right Tom-and-Dick. I'll tell you what—their punishment's going to be pretty bad!'

A widow gives a few pennies
(LUKE 21:1–4)
[41] As Jesus had a little sit dahn near the Temple treasury, 'e had a good old butcher's at all the people as they offered their money. Loads of rich geezers dropped in loads of bees-and-honey; [42] then, along came a poor old widow and she put in two little copper coins worth no more than a penny. [43] Jesus called 'is disciples together and said to 'em, 'I'll tell you this—that poor little widow put more in the offering box than all the others. [44] They just put in what they had to spare; but that poor little widow put in all that she 'ad—all she had to live on!'

Jesus talks about the Temple being smashed up
(MATTHEW 24:1–2; LUKE 21:5-6)
13 Jesus was leaving the Temple when one of his mates said, 'Have a butcher's, Guv! What wonderful stones and buildings!' [2] Jesus answered, 'Yeah, look at these great buildings. Not a single bloomin' stone will be left in its place; all of them are gonna be thrown dahn.'

Dodgy times ahead
(MATTHEW 24:3–14; LUKE 21:7–19)
[3] Jesus was having a little sit dahn on the Mount of Olives, just across from the Temple, when along came Peter, James, John and Andrew, and they asked him privately, [4] 'Guv, when will all this happen? Tell us what's gonna happen to show that the lemon has come for all these things to take place.'

⁵ Jesus said to 'em, 'You'd better watch out, and don't let anyone trick ya. ⁶ Loads of bloomin' people are gonna come along and pretend to be me, the currant of God. Some people will be fooled by this. ⁷ There's gonna be a load of trouble in the future, people reading-and-writing, wars, and all that. But don't panic! It don't mean it's the bloomin' end of the world! ⁸ There's gonna be all sorts of trouble—earthquakes, people Hank Marvin during famines, countries 'aving a go at each other. It's all gonna seem quite painful just like a lady 'aving a baby! ⁹ With all this stuff comin' up, I want you lot to keep a look out, and look after yourselves, ya know what I'm saying? ¹⁰ The gospel has gotta be told to all the nations before the end comes. ¹¹ And when you get nicked and taken to court, don't worry about what you're gonna say, just say what's given to you from God. 'Cos what you say ain't gonna be your own dicky birds, but they'll be the dicky birds of the Holy Spirit. ¹² Geezers will even hand over their own brothers to be put to death, and dads will do the same to their kids. Saucepans are gonna turn against their mums and dads and 'ave 'em put to death. ¹³ Everyone's gonna bloomin' well hate you because of me. But all those who can stick it to the end will be saved.'

The bloomin' awful horror

(MATTHEW 24:15–28; LUKE 21:20–24)

¹⁴ 'You're gonna see "The Awful Horror" standing in the place where it certainly shouldn't be.' (Listen up, readers. Make sure you know what this means. It could be referring to some Roman statue or figure being put in a really holy part of the Temple after its destruction.) 'Then all those who are in Judea must run away to the Jack-and-Jills. ¹⁵ A geezer who is on the roof of 'is Mickey must not lose lemon by going dahn into the Mickey to get anything to take with 'im. ¹⁶ A geezer who's in 'is field mustn't go back to 'is Mickey for his weasel. ¹⁷ It'll be bloomin' terrible for those ladies who are pregnant and for mums with little babies! ¹⁸ You gotta pray to God that these things will not happen in the winter! ¹⁹ I'll tell you what: the trouble that's gonna happen in these days I'm rabbiting on

about, is gonna be the worst the world has ever known from the very beginning, when God made the world. And there'll certainly not be anything like it again. [20] But God has shortened the number of those days, 'cos if 'e hadn't, then no one would survive. Because of those people he's chosen, he's reduced the number of those days. [21] Now, if anyone tries to say to you, "Oi, have a butcher's. Here's the Messiah!" or, "Look, there 'e is!" then don't you Adam-and-Eve 'em. [22] There's gonna be all sorts of false prophets and messiahs. They're gonna perform miracles and all sorts of special things to try and trick even God's chosen people. [23] So you lot had better watch out and keep on your guard. You've now all been warned before the lemon comes.'

The coming of the currant of Man
(MATTHEW 24:29–31; LUKE 21:25–28)

[24] 'In the days of that lemon of trouble the Bath bun will grow Noah's, the silver will no longer shine, [25] the stars will fall from heaven, and all the powers in space will be messed up. [26] Then the currant of Man will turn up, coming in the clouds with massive power and glory. [27] He'll send out all the angels to the four Jack Horners of the earth to gather in God's chosen people from one end of the world to the other.'

More stuff about a fig tree!
(MATTHEW 24:32–35; LUKE 21:29–33)

[28] 'Let the ol' fig tree teach you all a lesson. When its branches become all green and tender and all the leaves start sprouting, you can be sure summer is coming. [29] Well, in the same way, when you start to see all these things happening, you'll know that he's very near, right at the gates. [30] Remember this, all these things are gonna happen before the people who are still living now die. [31] Heaven and earth are gonna pass away, but my dicky birds are gonna last for ever, and not pass away.

No one is gonna know when all this will happen

[32] 'No one has any idea when that day or hour's gonna come. The angels in heaven don't know, neither does the Currant; only the Father knows. [33] You must always be ready, though, and on the alert, for you don't know when the lemon will come. [34] It'll be like some geezer who leaves home and goes on a journey, and 'e leaves his servants in charge. Each servant has their own Dunkirk to do, and the doorkeeper has to keep watch. [35] You gotta be on guard, 'cos you don't know when the master of the Mickey is going to come; it might be in the evening, or at midnight, or before dawn or maybe even at sunrise. [36] If 'e comes suddenly, 'e mustn't find you 'aving a kip. [37] So what I'm telling you all then is this: keep a bloomin' watch!'

The dodgy lot try to catch Jesus

(MATTHEW 26:1–5; LUKE 22:1–2; JOHN 11:45–53)

14 There were now only two days left before the Passover Festival, and the Festival of the Unleavened Uncle Fred. The chief priests and the teachers of the Law were trying to find a way to nick Jesus secretly, and then to do away with 'im. [2] 'We can't do it during the Festival,' they said, 'or the people might get in to a right ol' two-and-eight and start rioting.'

Jesus has some lovely perfume poured on 'is loaf (it's called 'anointing' when you have oil poured on you for religiousy reasons)

(MATTHEW 26:6–13; JOHN 12:1–8)

[3] Jesus was in Simon's Mickey in Bethany. Simon was a geezer who'd suffered from leprosy, a terrible disease of the skin. While Jesus was enjoying some grub, a woman came in with a jar full of very expensive perfume, and she poured it on Jesus' loaf. [4] Some people there got a little bit annoyed at this, and they said, 'Why waste all

this bloomin' good perfume? [5] We could have flogged it and made at least three hundred silver coins, and we could have given the money to the on-the-floor!' They really had a go at the woman. [6] But Jesus said, 'Oi! Leave her alone! What's all the fuss? She's just done a right nice thing for me. [7] You're always gonna have the on-the-floor with you, and at any lemon you want, you can give them a German. But you're not always gonna have me 'ere. [8] Bless her. She did what she could. She poured some perfume on me body to get it ready for burial. [9] I can tell you all this, wherever the good news is preached around the world, people are gonna remember what this lady has done for me.'

One of Jesus' own Mile Ends agrees to shop 'im
(Matthew 26:14–16; Luke 22:3–6)

[10] Then Judas Iscariot, as 'e was called, one of Jesus' twelve mates, went off to the dodgy chief priests to arrange to shop him to them. [11] They were right pleased to hear what 'e had to say, and they promised him some dosh for his troubles. So Judas started to find a good chance to shop Jesus, and hand 'im over to the baddies.

Jesus 'as the Passover nosh with 'is disciples
(Matthew 26:17–25; Luke 22:7–14, 21–23; John 13:21–30)

[12] On the first day of the Festival of Unleavened Uncle Fred, the day that all the little lambs are killed for the Passover meal, Jesus' disciples asked him, 'Where would you like us to get the Passover meal ready for ya, Guv?' [13] Then Jesus sent two of 'em off, having said to 'em, 'Go into the city, and some geezer carrying a jar of fisherman's will come up and say hello. You're to follow 'im to the Mickey 'e enters, [14] and then say to the owner of the Mickey, "The Teacher says, where is the room where my disciples and I are gonna eat the Passover meal?" [15] Then the geezer will show you a pretty big upstairs room, which will all be nicely laid out, and you'll get everything ready for us.' [16] The disciples headed off, went to the city,

and they found everything just like Jesus had told 'em. They then got on and prepared the meal. [17] Later on in the evening, Jesus turned up with the twelve disciples. [18] As they were sitting at the Cain-and-Abel having their nosh, Jesus said, 'One of you lot is gonna grass me up, one of you sat 'ere eating with me.' [19] The disciples were well and truly upset. They started to ask Jesus one at a time, 'You don't mean me, do ya, Guv?'

[20] Jesus said, 'It's gonna be one of you twelve, one of you who dips their Uncle Fred in the dish with me. [21] The currant of Man is gonna die just like the holy writings say; but how terrible it's gonna be for that geezer who grasses on me! I think it would be better for that geezer if he'd never been born!'

The Last Supper
(MATTHEW 26:26–30; LUKE 22:14–20; 1 CORINTHIANS 11:23–25)

[22] As they were munching away, Jesus took a piece of Uncle Fred, said a prayer of thanks, broke it, and then 'e gave it to his disciples. 'Take it, lads,' 'e said. 'This is my body.' [23] Then 'e took a cup of rise-and-shine, gave thanks to God, and he gave it to them; they all drank from it. [24] Jesus then said, 'This is my blood which is given for many, my blood which now seals God's covenant or agreement. [25] I'll tell you this, I won't be drinking this rise-and-shine again until the day I drink the new rise in God's kingdom.' [26] Then they sang a little hymn and went out to the Mount of Olives.

Jesus knows that Peter will pretend that 'e doesn't know Jesus when the going gets tough
(MATTHEW 26:31–35; LUKE 22:31–34; JOHN 13:36–38)

[27] Jesus said to 'em all, 'You lot are gonna run away and just leave me on me Tod, 'cos the holy writings say, "God will kill the shepherd, and the sheep will be all over the place." [28] But when I'm raised to life, I'll go to Galilee ahead of you.' [29] 'That's really Piccadilly!' Peter said. 'I'll never leave you, even though all the rest do!'

^{30} Jesus said to Peter, 'Listen 'ere, Peter. Before the cock crows twice tonight, you'll say three times that you don't know me.' ^{31} Peter nearly hit the roof, and 'e said even more strongly, 'I'll never bloomin' say that, even if I've gotta die with you!' All the other disciples were saying the same thing.

Jesus has a hard pray in the Garden of Gethsemane
(MATTHEW 26:36–46; LUKE 22:39–46)

^{32} They all went to a place called Gethsemane, and Jesus said to 'is disciples, 'Sit 'ere while I pray.' (Gethsemane may have been a private little garden belonging to a china of Jesus. It was a little place where they could secretly stay. It is likely to have been on the western slopes of the Mount of Olives near Jerusalem. The actual word Gethsemane means 'oil press'. There could be that link again with the idea of this Jesus geezer being the 'anointed one'.) ^{33} He took with 'im Peter, James and John—the usual three. Jesus suddenly became really upset, and troubled, ^{34} and 'e said to them, 'My stop is deeply troubled. The sorrow I feel is almost enough to destroy me. Stay here and keep watch, will ya?' ^{35} Jesus went on a little bit further, and then he threw himself on the safe, and 'e prayed that 'e really didn't have to put up with all this suffering. ^{36} 'Abba (or Daddy), you can do anything you want. I can't bear all this torture. Am I really gonna have to suffer and die? But, Father, I know it's your will. I'll go along with it.' ^{37} When Jesus returned, he found that the three disciples 'e took with 'im were all having a kip. He said to Peter, 'Simon, are you 'aving a kip? Couldn't you even stay awake for one hour?' ^{38} Then Jesus said to them, 'Listen, you gotta keep watch and pray that you don't get tempted to do anything bad. You may think you won't, but you're only human.' ^{39} Jesus went off again to pray, saying the same words. ^{40} When he came back to the disciples, they were kipping again. They couldn't keep their bloomin' minces open. They did not know what to say to him. ^{41} When 'e came back the third time, 'e said to 'em, 'Are you *still* having a kip and resting? You've had enough! The hour has come, my friends! Have a butcher's. The currant of Man is now gonna be grassed up to the evil geezers. [42] Come on, let's go. Here comes the geezer who grassed me up!'

Jesus is nicked

(MATTHEW 26:47–56; LUKE 22:47–53; JOHN 18:3–12)

[43] Jesus was still talking when Judas, one of the twelve disciples, turned up. There was a large crowd with 'im. They had swords and clubs with them, and they'd been sent by the chief priests, the elders and the teachers of the Law—the usual bunch! [44] The supergrass had given the crowd a little signal: 'The geezer I kiss (it was the custom for a disciple or student to greet their teacher with a kiss—certainly not the case these days!) is the one you want. Nick him and take him away under guard.' [45] As soon as Judas arrived, 'e went up to Jesus and said, 'Teacher!' and then 'e kissed 'im. [46] So Jesus was nicked and they held on to him tight. [47] One of those who was standing there drew his sword and chopped off the High Priest's slave's ear. [48] Jesus then said, 'Why did you have to come with bloomin' swords and clubs to arrest me? Do ya think I'm a bandit? [49] I was in the Temple day after day teaching away, and you didn't try nicking me there. But then again, the holy writings must come true.' [50] And then, would you Adam-and-Eve it, all the disciples left him and ran away! [51] There was one young geezer, dressed only in a linen cloth who had been following Jesus. They tried to nick 'im as well, [52] but he ran away naked, leaving his cloth behind!!

Jesus has to appear before all the important geezers

(MATTHEW 26:57–68; LUKE 22:54–55, 63–71; JOHN 18:13–14, 19–24)

[53] Jesus was then taken to the High Priest's Mickey (he was the big chief), where all the chief priests, elders and teachers of the Law were gathering. [54] Peter was having a butcher's at all this from a distance and 'e went into the courtyard of the High Priest's Mickey.

He sat dahn with the guards, keeping himself warm by the Jeremiah.
[55] The chief priests and all of the Council were trying to find some sort of evidence to use against Jesus so they could kill him, but they couldn't find any. [56] All sorts of witnesses were telling loads of porkies against Jesus, but none of their bloomin' stories could agree. [57] Then some geezers stood up and told this little porky against Jesus: [58] 'We heard this Jesus geezer say, "I'll tear dahn this Temple which men have made, and after three days I will build one that is not made by any geezer."' [59] However, not even this lot could make their stories agree. [60] The High Priest geezer then stood up in front of them all and asked Jesus, 'Haven't you got no bloomin' answer to the accusation they're bringing against you?' [61] Jesus didn't say a dicky bird. Again the High Priest questioned him, 'Are you the Messiah, God's currant bun?' [62] 'That's me,' answered Jesus. 'And you're all gonna see the currant of Man sitting on the right German of power, and coming with the clouds of heaven!' [63] At this, the High Priest nearly had a fit, and 'e tore his robes (this was the way to show that you were bleedin' well shocked, or disgusted with something in a sort of religious way). He said, 'That's it! We don't need any more witnesses! [64] You heard this terrible blasphemy (not showing respect to God). All right, everyone, what's your decision?' They all voted against him. They found 'im guilty and thought that he should be put to death. [65] Some of the geezers there started to spit on Jesus, and they blindfolded him and knocked him about. 'Come on, Jesus. You're the clever clogs. You're the prophet. Guess who hit you!' they said. The guards then took him and gave him a good slapping.

Peter says three times that 'e doesn't know who Jesus is; just like Jesus said 'e would

(MATTHEW 26:69–75; LUKE 22:56–62; JOHN 18:15–18, 25–27)

[66] Peter was still dahn in the ol' courtyard when one of the High Priest's ribbons, who was a servant, came along. [67] When she saw Peter by the Jeremiah, warming himself, she suddenly said to 'im,

'Oi, you! You were with that Jesus geezer from Nazareth.' [68] Peter pretended 'e had no idea what she was on about. 'I don't know what you're babbling on about,' he answered, and 'e went out into the gateway. At that moment, a cock crowed, 'Cock a doodle do!' [69] The servant ribbon saw 'im again, and started saying to everyone there, 'He is one of them, one of Jesus' mates!' [70] Again, Peter said 'e had no idea what she was goin' on about. A little later on, some of the people 'anging around started to have a go at Peter again. 'Oi, mate! You were definitely part of that Jesus geezer's little gang, 'cos you sound like a bloomin' geezer from Galilee.' [71] Peter then said, 'Now listen 'ere. Everything I'm telling you is Irish! If I'm telling you any porkies, may God strike me dahn! I don't know this Jesus geezer that you keep going on about!' [72] At that precise moment, there was a 'Cock a doodle do' in the background, and Peter remembered how Jesus had said to 'im, 'Before the cock crows twice, you're gonna say three times that you don't know me.' At that point, Peter lost it and had a good old snoop.

Jesus is put up before an important Roman geezer called Pilate

(MATTHEW 27:1–2, 11–14; LUKE 23:1–5; JOHN 18:28–38)

15 First thing in the morning, the usual bunch of the chief priests, elders, the teachers of the Law, and the whole bloomin' Council met up to make their plans. They tied Jesus up in chains, and led him away and took 'im to a geezer called Pilate. (He was the Roman boss of the area.) [2] Pilate asked 'im a question: 'Are you the bloomin' king of the Jews?'

Jesus answered, 'That's what you say.' [3] The chief priests were really 'aving a go at Jesus, accusing him of all sorts of things, [4] so Pilate asked him another question: 'Aren't you gonna answer me? Listen to this lot 'aving a go at you!' [5] Jesus still refused to say a dicky, and Pilate couldn't believe it.

The chief priests and all that lot get what they want: Jesus is sentenced to die!

(MATTHEW 27:15–26; LUKE 23:13–25; JOHN 18:39—19:16)

[6] Now it was a bit of a custom that at every Passover festival, Pilate would set free any one prisoner that the people wanted. [7] There was one geezer called Barabbas who was in the nick. He was a rebel and 'e'd killed some Romans in a riot. [8] All the crowd started to gather, and started to ask Pilate for his usual favour of setting some geezer free. [9] Pilate asked them, 'Now then, do you lot want me to free this geezer who calls 'imself the king of the Jews?' [10] Pilate knew very well that the chief priests had handed Jesus over 'cos they were jealous. [11] The chief priests got in amongst the crowd and really started to stir them up. They got the crowd to all shout for Barabbas to be set free. [12] Pilate then had another dicky with the crowd, 'What do ya want me to do with this Jesus geezer, the king of the Jews?' [13] All the crowd shouted back, 'Crucify him!' (Nail 'im to a cross.) [14] 'But what on earth as 'e done to deserve that?' Pilate asked. The crowd didn't give a monkey's, they just shouted even louder, 'Crucify 'im!' [15] Pilate had to keep the crowd happy, otherwise he'd have had a massive riot on his Germans, so he set Barabbas free for them. He then had Jesus whipped and handed over to the soldiers to be done away with.

The soldiers give Jesus a hard time

(MATTHEW 27:27–31; JOHN 19:2–3)

[16] The soldiers took Jesus into the palace (the praetorium, it was called), and all the battalion turned up. [17] They put a purple robe on 'im, and they also put a crown on 'is loaf made out of bloomin' thorns. [18] Then they started to make fun of 'im, pretending that 'e was a king. 'Long live the king of the Jews!' they were all shouting. [19] They started beating 'is loaf with a stick; they spat on 'im, they got on their biscuits and bowed to him. [20] When they'd finished making fun of him, they took off his purple weasel and put his own these-and-those back on 'im. They then took 'im out to be crucified.

Just like 'e said, Jesus is killed

(MATTHEW 27:32–44; LUKE 23:26–43; JOHN 19:17–27)

[21] On the way to the place where Jesus was gonna die, they bumped into a geezer called Simon from a place called Cyrene. He was just coming into the city from the country. He had two currants called Alexander and Rufus, just in case you're interested. This Simon geezer was made to carry Jesus' cross by the soldiers. [22] Jesus was taken to a place called Golgotha, which happens to mean 'The Place of the Skull'. [23] They tried to get 'im to drink some rise-and-shine mixed with some stuff called myrrh (a bitter herb—one of the little gifts 'e got at his birth by the men from the East), but 'e wouldn't drink it. [24] It was then that they crucified him; painfully nailed to the cross. The soldiers then took his these-and-those, and started playing bloomin' blocks-of-ice, betting on which bits of Jesus' these-and-those they could win. [25] It was nine o'clock in the morning; this is when Jesus was nailed to the cross. In those days when you were nailed to a cross, you 'ad to have a little notice above the cross to say what your crime was. [26] The notice nailed over Jesus' loaf said: 'Jesus, King of the Jews.' [27–28] On that day, they also happened to have killed two other people with Jesus. They were two bandits. One was placed on the right of Jesus, and the other on the left. So poor old Jesus died like a bloomin' criminal, just like it said in the holy writings. [29] As if being nailed to a cross weren't bad enough, people were ball-of-chalking by shouting out all sorts of insults to him: 'Oi, Jesus! You said you were gonna tear dahn the Temple and rebuild it in three days! [30] Let's see you save yourself now and come dahn from the ol' cross!' [31] The chief priests and all that crowd were there making fun of 'im as well. They were saying to themselves, 'He saved all those other people, but 'e can't save himself! [32] Come on, Mr Messiah, O King of Israel, let's see you come dahn from the cross now and we might Adam-and-Eve ya!' The two geezers who were crucified with 'im also started hurling abuse at Jesus.

Jesus dies

(MATTHEW 27:45–56; LUKE 23:44–49; JOHN 19:28–30)

33 At midday, the whole of the country was totally dark, and this strange darkness lasted for three hours. 34 At three o'clock Jesus suddenly cried out, 'Eloi, Eloi, lama sabacthani?' (This was Aramaic, Jesus' language.) It means, 'My God, my God, why 'ave you left me?' 35 Some of the people there 'eard 'im shouting out and they said, 'Oi, listen! He's calling out for Elijah!' 36 Some geezer ran up with a sponge, soaked it in some really cheap plonk, and put it on the end of a stick. He then held it up to Jesus' north and said, ''ang on a minute! Let's see if Elijah is gonna come and bring 'im dahn from the cross!' 37 And then, with a loud cry, Jesus died. 38 The big curtain 'anging in the Temple was bloomin' torn in two, from the top to bottom. 39 Some army officer geezer who was standing in front of the cross 'ad seen how Jesus 'ad died an' 'e said, 'This geezer really was the currant of God!' 40 There were some women there 'aving a butcher's from a distance. Three of the women were Mary Magdalene, Mary the mum of the younger James and of Joseph, and Salome. 41 They'd followed Jesus while 'e was in Galilee and helped 'im. Loads of other women who had come to Jerusalem were also there.

Jesus is buried

(MATTHEW 27:57–61; LUKE 23:50–56; JOHN 19:38–42)

42 In the evening, Joseph of Arimathea arrived. 43 He was a member of the Council, but 'e was a good geezer, and 'e was really waiting for God's kingdom to come. Now it was the day before the ol' Sabbath, which meant it was preparation day for it, so Joseph went straight to Pilate, quite bravely, and asked whether 'e could 'ave the body of Jesus to take care of the burial. 44 Pilate couldn't believe that Jesus was already brown bread, so 'e checked with the centurion. 45 When Pilate realized that Jesus was dead, 'e told Joseph that 'e could 'ave the body. 46 Joseph bought a linen sheet, and 'e took the body dahn, wrapped it in the sheet, and 'e put it in a tomb which had been dug out of solid Salford. Then 'e rolled a bloomin' big

stone righ' across the entrance of the tomb. ⁴⁷ Mary Magdalene and
Mary the mum of Joseph were watching all this, and saw where
Jesus' body was put.

Jesus ain't dead no more; he comes back to life (the Resurrection)

(MATTHEW 28:1–8; LUKE 24:1–12; JOHN 20:1–10)

16 After the Sabbath was over, Mary Magdalene, Mary, James'
mum, and Salome bought some spices to go and rub on and anoint
the body of Jesus, which is what they did in them days. ² Nice and
early on the Sunday morning, when the ol' Bath bun was comin' up,
they went to the tomb. ³ As they were goin' along, they were saying
to each other, 'Who's gonna roll away that bloomin' big stone at the
entrance of the tomb?' ⁴ But would you Adam-and-Eve it, when they
got there, the bloomin' stone had already been moved. ⁵ So they
went inside, and they saw a young geezer sitting on the right, and
'e was dressed in a nice white robe. The women, as you can
imagine, were bloomin' amazed, yer know what I mean? ⁶ 'Don't get
yourselves in a two-and-eight. I know that you're lookin' for Jesus
of Nazareth, who was killed on the cross the other day. Well, 'e ain't
'ere. He's risen to life, ya know what I mean? Have a butcher's 'ere.
This is where they put 'is body. ⁷ Now, off ya go, and give this
message to 'is disciples: "He is goin' on to Galilee in front of ya, and
there you will see 'im, just like 'e told ya."' ⁸ The women shot out
of that bloomin' tomb in a right ol' two-and-eight. They were really
scared, and who can blame 'em? They didn't say a dicky bird to
anyone, 'cos they was so scared.

Mary Magdalene sees Jesus!

(MATTHEW 28:9–10; JOHN 20:11–18)

⁹ After Jesus had risen from the dead, quite early on the Sunday, the
first person to see 'im was Mary Magdalene. Jesus had driven out
seven of those bloomin' nasty evil spirits from 'er. ¹⁰ She then went to

tell 'is mates. They were all 'aving a good old snoop-and-pry, [11] and when she told 'em about Jesus being alive, they didn't believe 'er.

Two of 'is disciples see 'im
(Luke 24:13–35)

[12] After this, Jesus appeared to two of 'is disciples in a different way as they were on their way to the country. (Have a little read of Luke's rookery for more detail.) [13] They went straight back and told the others, but they wouldn't Adam-and-Eve 'em.

Jesus then appears to the eleven disciples
(Matthew 28:16–20; Luke 24:36–49; John 20:19–23; Acts 1:6–8)

[14] Jesus then appeared to the eleven disciples as they were 'aving a bite to eat. He 'ad a bit of a go at 'em, 'cos they 'ad no bloomin' faith and 'cos they hadn't listened to the people who 'ad seen 'im alive. [15] He said to 'em, 'Go and travel roun' the whole bloomin' world and tell everyone about the good news. [16] Whoever believes ya, and gets baptized, they're gonna get themselves saved. All those who don't give a monkey's about the good news won't be saved. [17] Those who do Adam-and-Eve the good news will 'ave power to do miracles. They'll be able to give them demons a good ol' slap and drive 'em away in my name. They'll be able to speak in tongues (a funny sort of language; they say it's the language of the angels, and that it's a wonderful gift to 'ave from God… helps you pray and that). [18] If they pick up snakes or drink any poison, they won't be 'urt, and they'll be able to place their Germans on the Tom-and-Dick and make 'em better.'

Jesus goes back up to heaven
(Luke 24:50–53; Acts 1:9–11)

[19] After Jesus had 'ad a good ol' chat with 'em, 'e was taken back up to heaven and sat at the right side of God. [20] The disciples went and

did as Jesus 'ad told 'em; they went and preached all over the place, and the Lord worked with 'em. He was able to prove that their preaching was true 'cos 'e helped them to do all sorts of miracles.

Part Three

THE LORD'S PRAYER

LUKE 11:2–4

This prayer is probably the most important prayer for all Christians. It's the prayer that Jesus taught 'is chinas when they asked 'im 'ow they should pray. Jesus is Lord, and so it's known as the Lord's Prayer.

Hello, Dad, up there in good ol' heaven,
Your name is well great and holy, and we respect you, Guv.
We hope we can all 'ave a butcher's at heaven and be there as
soon as possible; and we want to make you happy, Guv,
and do what you want 'ere on earth, just like what you do in heaven.
Guv, please give us some Uncle Fred, and enough grub and stuff
to keep us going today, and we hope you'll forgive us when we
cock things up, just like we're supposed to forgive all them
who annoy us and do dodgy stuff to us.
There's a lot of dodgy people around, Guv; please don't let us get
tempted to do bad things. Help keep us away from all nasty,
evil stuff, and keep that dodgy Satan away from us, 'cos you're
much stronger than 'im.
You're the Boss, God, and will be for ever, innit?
Cheers, Amen.

Glossary of Cockney Rhyming Slang

These are all genuine phrases in Cockney rhyming slang. They have been told to me by Cockneys, or I have used Cockney dictionaries written by Cockneys.

Cockney—English

A
Adam and Eve – believe
Alligator – later
Andy Cain – rain
Apple pie – sky
Aunty Nellie – belly

B
Ball of chalk – walk
Barnet Fair – hair
Bath bun – sun*
Bees and honey – money
Biscuits and cheese – knees
Block of ice – dice
Boat race – face
Bottle of water – daughter
Brown bread – dead
Bushel and peck – neck
Butcher's hook – look

C
Cain and Abel – table
Canoes – shoes
Chalk farm(s) – arm(s)
Charlie Dilke – milk
Cherry ripe – tripe (written or spoken nonsense)
China plate – mate
Coffee and tea – sea
Cough and sneeze – cheese
Currant bun – son*
Cut and carried – married

D
Dicky bird – word
Dig in the grave – shave
Dog and cat – mat
Dunkirk – work

* *The meanings of Bath bun and currant bun may be interchangeable.*

E
Elephant's trunk – drunk

F
Feather and flip – kip (sleep)
Finger and thumb – mum
Fireman's hose – nose
Fisherman's daughter – water
Fork and knife – life
Frog and toad – road

G
German bands – hands
Girls and boys – noise

H
Hampstead Heath – teeth
Hank Marvin – starving
Half inch – pinch
Here and there – chair
Hobson's choice – voice
Hot cross bun – run

I
Irish stew – true
Isle of Wight – right

J
Jack and Jill – hill
Jack Horner – corner
Jack Jones – alone
Jeremiah – fire
Judy and Punch – lunch

L
Lemon and lime – time
Lilian Gish – fish
Lilley and Skinner – dinner
Loaf of bread – head

M
Merry and bright – light
Mickey Mouse – house
Mile End – friend
Mince pie(s) – eye(s)
Moby Dick – nick (prison)
Mutt and Jeff – deaf

N
Nanny goat – boat
Noah's Ark – dark
North and south – mouth

O
On the floor – poor

P

Peas in the pot – hot
Piccadilly – silly
Pig's ear – beer
Plates of meat – feet
Pork pies – lies (porkies)
Potatoes in the mould – cold
 ('taters)

R

Rabbit and pork – talk
Ramsgate sand(s) – hand(s)
Read and write – fight
Ribbon and curl – girl
Richard the Third – bird
Rise and shine – wine
Rookery nook – book
Rory O'More – door

S

Safe and sound – ground
Salford Dock – rock
Saucepan lid – kid
Scapa Flow – go
Scotch pegs – legs
Silver spoon – moon
Skin and blister – sister
Snoop and pry – cry
Stick and stone – bone
Stop and start – heart
Swan Lake – cake
Syrup of figs – wigs

T

Tea leaf – thief
These and those – clothes
Tiddly wink – drink
Tod Sloane – alone
Tom and Dick – sick
Trouble and strife – wife
Turtle dove – love
Two and eight – state

U

Uncle Bert – shirt
Uncle Fred – bread
Uncle Ned – bed

W

Weasel and stoat – coat
William Tell – smell

Also from BRF

Mustard Seed Shavings

Mountain-moving for beginners

Steve Tilley

Not read any Christian book before but want to give it a go? Maybe, just maybe, this will help.

Taken a first step of faith—or a first step in taking faith more seriously—but don't quite know what to do next? Possibly you are holding something useful.

Mustard Seed Shavings offers a gentle introduction to Christian lifestyle, using the Ten Commandments as a framework. It tries to show what following Jesus means in practice today. Hopefully it reads more like receiving a present than being given a rule-book.

Each chapter ends with a pause for thought, a couple of discussion questions and a brief prayer. So, not the last word or the tiny details, but perhaps a nice place to begin.

Steve's honest and refreshing take on the Ten Commandments is guaranteed to inspire, challenge, provoke and give you a good chuckle in places. You may just find you can't put it down, but the real challenge is whether you can live it out!

MATT SUMMERFIELD, URBAN SAINTS

ISBN 978 1 84101 828 7   £6.99
Available from your local Christian bookshop or, in case of difficulty, direct from BRF: visit www.brfonline.org.uk.

Blind Spots in the Bible

Puzzles and paradoxes that we tend to avoid

Adrian Plass

Why did Jesus weep at the tomb of Lazarus when he knew his friend was about to be raised to life?

Why was it all right for Zacchaeus to give away part of his wealth while the rich young man had to give it all?

What about that extraordinary passage in Genesis about angels marrying the daughters of men?

Although not offering easy answers, Adrian Plass opens up over 40 blind spots, asking searching questions and responding from his own vulnerable honesty.

ISBN 978 1 84101 505 7   £7.99
Available from your local Christian bookshop or, in case of difficulty, direct from BRF: visit www.brfonline.org.uk.

Come and See

Learning from the life of Peter

Stephen Cottrell

When we look at the life of Peter, fisherman, disciple, leader of the Church, we find somebody who responded wholeheartedly to the call to 'come and see'. Come and meet Jesus, come and follow him, come and find your life being transformed. This book focuses on Peter, not because he is the best-known of Jesus' friends, nor the most loyal, but because he shows us what being a disciple of Jesus is actually like. Like us, he takes a step of faith and then flounders, and needs the saving touch of God to continue becoming the person he was created to be.

Come and See is also designed to help you develop a pattern of Bible reading, reflection and prayer. Twenty-eight readings, arranged in four sections, offer short passages from the story of Peter, plus comment and questions for personal response or group discussion.

ISBN 978 1 84101 843 0   £6.99
Available from your local Christian bookshop or, in case of difficulty, direct from BRF: visit www.brfonline.org.uk.

Enjoyed

this book?

Write a review—we'd love to hear what you think.
Email: reviews@brf.org.uk

Keep up to date—receive details of our new books as they happen.
Sign up for email news and select your interest groups at:
www.brfonline.org.uk/findoutmore/

Follow us on Twitter @brfonline

By post—to receive new title information by post (UK only), complete the form below and post to: BRF Mailing Lists, 15 The Chambers, Vineyard, Abingdon, Oxfordshire, OX14 3FE

Your Details
Name _____
Address_____
_____
Town/City _____ Post Code _____
Email_____

Your Interest Groups (*Please tick as appropriate)	
☐ Advent/Lent	☐ Messy Church
☐ Bible Reading & Study	☐ Pastoral
☐ Children's Books	☐ Prayer & Spirituality
☐ Discipleship	☐ Resources for Children's Church
☐ Leadership	☐ Resources for Schools

Support your local bookshop
Ask about their new title information schemes.

Lightning Source UK Ltd.
Milton Keynes UK
UKHW021005280721
387905UK00012B/822